Growing Old in America

Book Three
1996-2021

By
Walt Filkowski

Copyright 2020 by Walt Filkowski

Growing Old in America
Published by Yawn's Publishing
2555 Marietta Hwy, Suite 103
Canton, GA 30114
www.yawnsbooks.com

All rights reserved. No part of this book may be reproduced or transmitted in any form, electronic or mechanical, including photocopying, recording, or data storage systems without the express written permission of the publisher, except for brief quotations in reviews and articles.

Library of Congress Control Number: 2021903036

ISBN13: 978-1-954617-05-6

Printed in the United States

CONTENTS

Prologue	i
The Aging Process	1
The Search	4
Innkeepers at Last	21
What Planet Is Mercersburg, PA On?	28
Mercersburg Academy	34
Prospect	36
A Family Again	38
The First Major Crisis	41
The First Major Mistake	44
Visitors	48
Notable Guests	64
Community Involvement	79
Inn Pets	85
Designated Inn Storyteller	89
Burned Out or Just Bored	94
Raising A Child in Your Place Of Business	101
Final Days	109
Life In Big Canoe	116

What Was A Big Canoe?	120
Motorcycle Time	127
Another New Career	133
Not All Work and No Play	143
"Death Takes A Holiday" But Not in Big Canoe	151
The Final Move	152
Plan B	157
Sandarlin Mountain	160
Welcome to Soleil	163
Final Days in Soleil	181
Life Begins at Eighty	189
Pandemic	195
The End of The Book (Not Me)	202
Epilogue	205

Growing Old in America

PROLOGUE

This will be the final book of the "America" trilogy, written for my immediate family that has memorialized my existence over ten decades, starting with my birth in 1939. All three books are my recollection of events and milestones in my life and, as I have already been told, might be perceived differently by others. I never really knew much about my parents or grandparents growing up, or even today. One of my daughters, Dana, suggested once after hearing all the old college stories at my 70th birthday party, attended by my college roommates, that I should "write this stuff down" before Alzheimer's sets in, and so here you have the final chapter. As soon as I got current on historical events, this book became more of a diary as the story continued. Thus, a work in progress became the theme.

The first book of the trilogy, "Growing up in America", concerned itself with memories of experiences and the resulting choices most of my generation made after having had these experiences, in what has been called the last generation of innocence. Dealing with siblings, making and breaking friendships, sports or no sports, dealing with the opposite sex, handling discipline, smoking, alcohol (drugs were not a factor at this point), independence, driver's license, the first car, and the big one, education. In my situation, most choices were made by me alone, but I know in some situations choices were made by my parents and/or oldest sister. Choices sometimes changed with more experience, and it did in my case. I turned my back on education in high school, but after three years in the Navy came back to it. Football may have had something to do with that particular decision, but not entirely.

The second book, "Making It in America", dealt primarily with career building and fulfilling the "American Dream" of two gender equity children, a house in the country with a swimming pool, and a fancy car. In my case, it included a college education following a stint in the Navy, and a post-graduate degree. I made some good choices during this period as well as some not so good ones. I experienced both the story book wedding and "American Dream", and the California divorce by age 39, which left me disillusioned and broke. There was such a thing as a second chance and I met my soul mate to whom I owe my continued existence today. Drugs were now readily available, but I was never interested. I smoked for a brief period and continued the pursuit of alcohol dating back from age 14 to this present day, but never in excess.

This brings us to the final book of the trilogy, "Growing Old in America". It has taken seven years, so far, to complete this final chapter in my life because it has proven to be a work in progress. I would not have imagined living to 81 plus, back in my college days, in the crazy world and country we live in today. We started out this chapter dropping out of our health care careers at our peak income years, in favor of a life care choice of owning and operating a Bed and Breakfast or Country Inn over money and career. Retirement turned out to be a "seven-twenty-four" existence, which I entered into too late in life, it turned out. Final retirement for me eight years later turned out to be a matter of health care. Growing old no matter where you live comes down to fighting the battle of a deteriorating body. The aging process is not kind to any aspect of the human body, and considerable time and expense is expended to defer and/or correct its effects. At the beginning of this book, I mention that one of the variables in growing old was how one took care of, or abused, his machine, or body. That will be the theme throughout "Growing Old in America".

THE AGING PROCESS

At what point does one begin to get old? Is it a physical process with the hips and knees going first, followed closely by the prostrate enlarging and the lens in your eye clouding over? Or is it the failing memory and slight tremor in the hands, followed by a decrease in sexual drive and an increase in sitting in front of the T.V? Do the parts quit working first, or does the brain that directs the parts malfunction initially? In some cases, it is both a mental and physical process brought on by a catastrophic health-related episode, i.e., a heart attack or stroke.

Geriatricians prefer to say that growing old is "in the mind of the beholder," with some people "aging" faster than others, depending on a long list of variables.

Some of those variables include; how well you took care of, or abused, your body, diet, genetics, occupation, and mental disposition. I was taking Anatomy in college about the time I suffered my third severe concussion and began comparing my body to a machine; with my brain being the computer that ran the whole show. At that point, I felt a need to beef up my support structure to protect what was left of my computer; and put on forty pounds of muscle with a weight-lifting program. I did not maintain this protective bulk, however, but did manage to avoid further injury to my computer-brain over the next few years of playing football. Unfortunately, other parts of my "machine" did not fare too well.

My heart was the pump that drove a hydraulic system (circulatory system) that operated my appendages, and my brain (computer) supplied the electrical system (nervous system) that energized everything. Fuel was supplied by my digestive system and extraneous plumbing functions were carried out by my kidneys and colon. I could almost equate every bodily function to a machine function, with a few exceptions of course. I even wrote a paper on it for a Kinesiology class later on, but the Ph.D. professor did not share my analogy.

    The aging process began for me in my mid-forties with a cataract in my left eye. It was too early for a geriatric cataract, but the ophthalmologist could not find a trauma- related incident that would have precipitated such an early defect. He dismissed my three football concussions and sunburned eyes in the Navy as a possible cause. Next came the benign enlarged prostrate in my early fifties, which scared me at the time, before I found out it was benign, because it put me right on schedule to kick the bucket around age 54. Even though my older brother was still alive and kicking and four years older than me, the fact that no male Filkowski had lived to see his 52nd birthday still haunted me. So, for all intent and purposes, my official aging process started with physical problems. These were mechanical problems and were handled as such, with surgical intervention and modern chemistry. A third problem presented itself when the eye doctor found I had glaucoma during a routine eye exam. Just as I had speculated that the prostrate problem may have been connected to having a vasectomy in my forties, I wondered out loud if the glaucoma was a result of the lens implant that corrected the cataract. I was unaware of any male in my family having either of these problems, with my older brother being the only one to have lived long enough to experience such anatomical defects.

    So, as my fifty-plus year old parts began to wear out I rationalized it by counting myself fortunate. Not many machines that were fifty years old were still running and those that were not maintained properly and/or abused were long gone. I had certainly physically abused my body with fourteen years of football, and an alcohol history dating back to when I was fourteen. I had developed a "heal thy self" mentality after my pneumonia experience in Navy boot camp, and not being able to afford health insurance during the next eight years in college. I had two old cars in college that developed mechanical problems which seemed to go away when I let the car sit for a while. I adopted that philosophy for my own health care up until I could afford health insurance, and even then, resorted to hallway consults with willing physicians when health issues came up.

When I left my job at Summit Medical Center at age fifty-four, and tried consulting for a year, my prostate problem was somewhat controlled by the drug Hytrin. There were still frequent trips to the restroom and roadside bushes, and my life would never be the same for some time to come. It was about this time we began the serious search for a Bed and Breakfast outside of California, with failing eyesight and a prostate the size of a softball.

Walt Filkowski

THE SEARCH

It has been said by some that the fun part of owning and operating a Bed and Breakfast is the search to find one for sale that fits your criteria. The search involved traveling around the country staying in these Inns and sampling their breakfasts, and sometimes dinners. At first, it was fun because Sandy and I did it together, but there were times her work schedule required me to do it solo, and after a while it became a chore.

By this time, after attending some conferences and living through the Benbow Inn experience, we knew it had to be at least eight to ten rooms with a high occupancy, upscale to generate high room rates, within ninety minutes of a metropolitan center of at least 100,000 population, and have some kind of tourist draw, i.e., beach, ski resort, historical area, etc. We always tried to coordinate a site visit with a business trip related to Sandy's work as CFO of a large catholic hospital in Santa Rosa, or my fledgling consulting activity in California. We had already exhausted most of the available properties in California as being too expensive or too small, and we still had our youngest child, Megan, to get through high school and college to consider, from a financial standpoint.

A complicating factor in the early 1990's was that the internet was not around yet and we had to rely on print media to find Inns for sale. Usually by the time we read about an available B&B in the hospitality magazines, the really good ones would have already sold. We also checked the real estate section of the Wall Street Journal for old mansions up for sale that could be turned into an Inn or B&B. The conferences we attended always had a real estate board set up that posted properties for sale and properties wanted. We could have written a book just on our experiences in looking at potential properties, and will relate a few on the following pages.

One of our early scouting trips coincided with an American

Hospital Association Annual Meeting in January of 1990 that was held over Super Bowl Sunday. It was memorable because the San Francisco 49ers beat the Denver Broncos 55 to 7, the most lopsided win in Super Bowl history. The meeting was held at the prestigious Four Seasons in Washington, D.C. and I was attending as a spouse of Sandy. Even in 1990, D.C. was a dangerous place and when I left the lobby to take a walk, I was warned not to venture more than two blocks from the hotel. The Board Chairman and some key physicians from Sandy's hospital were attending the meeting and her CEO instructed her to entertain them at the Inn at Little Washington, a five-star restaurant located about 60 minutes outside D.C. itself.

I was recruited to rent a car and drive the party out to the restaurant and back, and it worked out great that Sandy and I would both get to see this famous Inn and restaurant. I inquired about renting a car at the Concierge Desk and told them our destination and requested a car large enough to seat six comfortably. They made the arrangements and told me Enterprise would be bringing the car around at the appointed time, along with directions to the Inn. That night we all piled into a Cadillac sedan and took off for dinner at the Inn at Little Washington. I always scan the dashboard gauges whenever I drive because of the large number of clunker cars I owned growing up, in the service, and in college. For some reason, I could not find the gas gauge and no one else in the car could either. I asked my passenger in front of the glove compartment to look it up in the car manual and, about an hour into the drive, he located a little bar gauge that indicated we were just about out of gas.

By this time, it was dark and we were out in the boonies without a gas station in sight, and it would not have been prudent to run out of gas with a car full of hospital bigwigs. Fortunately, a mom-and-pop grocery store with a single gas pump showed up on the horizon and saved the day. Dinner at the Inn was fantastic and we got to peek in some of the rooms, which were equally fantastic. When we returned to the hotel, I immediately went to the Concierge Desk and asked the same person who arranged for the car how Enterprise could rent a car with an almost empty gas tank? He replied that most guests only use the car to drive around D.C. to see the sites so they only keep four gallons in the tank. When I reminded him that I had told him our destination, he just shrugged it off.

The next day I hopped a plane and flew down to Charleston, South Carolina, to look at an operating inn and a mansion with possibilities of becoming an inn. Neither proved viable, but the female real estate agent showing the properties made me an offer that Sandy would not have approved of.

On another scouting trip, we took advantage of Sandy attending a meeting in Philadelphia and looked at an old mansion in Holyoke, Massachusetts, and then traveled west over to Lenox to check out a couple of B&B's that were for sale. Lenox is where the Boston Pops orchestra spends the summer playing at Tanglewood, sort of a music camp with a big amphitheater. One of the properties was an old mansion that sat on a hill overlooking Tanglewood, and you could hear the music from the front porch. It was on three or four acres and had a separate house for owner's quarters, which we really liked, in addition to an old mansion with several guest rooms. It also had a two-story motel –type building on the property with motel-like rooms. Sandy liked the place because it made a ton of money with very little expense and was closed during the winter months. I was concerned about the old mansion, which was a fire trap with dead end corridors and spaghetti wiring in the basement. We found out from the realtor handling the sale that the owners were looking for a creative financial package because they would have a huge capital gains problem if they got their asking price. It was obvious from the condition of the property that they had not put much money into maintaining the place. The owners liked Sandy and her creative financial thinking and we pursued this property vigorously.

Sandy liked the little town of Lenox, mostly because it had a woman's clothing store, Talbot's, where she purchased an expensive dress on sale for $7.00. We left Lenox to drive down to Philadelphia, using Triple A's TripTicket program that gave us directions right to the hotel where Sandy's meeting was. The directions were literally line-of-sight and as the crow flies, which nearly proved disastrous.

We started south on three and four lane highways, then two-lane roads which turned into single-lane country roads and eventually a one-way inner-city road at night in a very black neighborhood. While sitting at a red light with the windows up and the doors locked, a police car stopped in the intersection and a white officer got out and approached our car. He asked what in the hell we were doing in this neighborhood and, after I explained about the TripTicket, he said to follow his car and not stop until he told us to. He took us right to the hotel and advised us to not rely on TripTicket without looking at a map also.

We kept in touch with the Lenox realtor almost daily while in Philadelphia and upon returning home to Santa Rosa, Sandy put together and forwarded a creative financial offer that softened the owner's capital gains issue. The realtor said the owners loved our offer and us (Sandy), but there was another buyer they would have to deal with first. He said it was not a ploy by the owners to get us to offer more money, but merely their need to deal with him since he was first in with an offer. The realtor would call us (no e-mail yet) every few days to assure us we were still no. 1, and then once a week, and then not at all. Our attempts at reaching the realtor, or the owner, proved fruitless until I decided to call him very early in the morning at home and he answered the phone still groggy from sleep. When pressed, he stated the Inn had sold, and when I asked if the first guy had bought it, he hemmed and hawed and finally admitted that he, the realtor, had purchased it. He had used Sandy's creative offer as his own when he saw how much money the property generated.

I hung up and called a Massachusetts attorney we had talked to about another property and explained the situation, thinking we had a good case. Wrong! He explained that Massachusetts was a Commonwealth, and in a Commonwealth a written contract is not worth the paper it is written on. He also reminded me that if this went to trial, the outcome would be determined by a jury of the agent's peers, and a California man accusing a local would not go over well. We knew this last revelation to be true in another attempt at buying an Inn in Maine. The lawyer advised us to "grin and bear it", and move on with our search, because we would end up spending a lot of time and money and gaining nothing when it was said and done.

The Maine incident was our version of the Spanish-American war battle cry of "Remember the Maine." We found this Inn, just outside Camden, Maine, listed for sale in a B&B magazine and booked the most expensive room, as I think it coincided with our wedding anniversary. It was a real castle filled with antiques in every nook and cranny of its eleven bedrooms and luxurious common space, and situated almost right on the ocean. There was also a separate house nearby, on what used to be the estate grounds, that was being sold separately and would have made a perfect owner's quarters. The owner was a man from California who also owned an old estate that sat on a hill above the castle. We worked with a real estate broker who represented the owner, and who shared a lot of information about the reasons for the sale. It seems the owner was a "typical California know it all" who had antagonized the locals with threats of lawsuits if he did not get his way, and the Inn was also losing money because he was never around to oversee the operation.

As serious buyers, we were given the operating financial reports and it did not take Sandy long to figure out why the place did not generate much of a profit. The owner was charging all of his expenses from both properties to the Inn, including frequent airline tickets to and from California. By discounting expense in an appropriate amount, Sandy was sure the Inn could turn a profit after debt service. The $2 million-dollar turnkey price was very reasonable considering the antique furnishings and location between highway 1 and the ocean. We made an offer at the listing price and met with the owner in the real estate office. Half way through the paperwork the owner reminded everyone the sales price did not include the furnishings and all hell broke loose. His own real estate agent yelled out that he had never said that and, as she tried to stand up, she fell back over her chair. Having to furnish a castle with antiques would be very expensive and a deal breaker. We said as much and stormed out of the office.

The realtor called us the next day and said that she thought the owner did not really want to sell the property, and had put it up for sale as a trial balloon to see what the interest was. We were crushed, as this was a premier property at a price we could have afforded and with a lot of potential for growth. It was not the last place we would visit that did not meet our expectations or even come close to what was stated in the listing.

Another Inn we found for sale in the print media was located in Springfield, Vermont. Vermont is the Mecca for B&B's and has over 400 of them because of the autumn leaf season and winter skiing. The ad showed an old mansion previously owned by a one-term Governor of the state, James Hartness, with beautiful gardens and a unique feature on the front lawn. It had a bar and restaurant, good financials and a high occupancy for its twenty plus rooms.

The town of Springfield turned out to be an old mill town full of abandoned and rusting factories from the 1920's era, and not much else. The Inn itself sat on a hill overlooking the town and was an imposing structure from the outside. It had fourteen guestrooms in the main house and another thirty-two-small motel-like rooms added on at the rear of the house, in two wings that wiped out most, if not all, of the once beautiful gardens pictured in the sales brochure. Leading up from the foyer was a beautiful oak staircase with a railing that was so rickety it was dangerous to use. We could not figure out what the draw was for people to come there as it was too far south for the leaves or skiing and the town was an eyesore. The unique feature on the front lawn was an astronomy domed observatory with an underground tunnel coming from the main house basement.

It was at dinner in the restaurant, and observing the large number of Japanese male guests, that we found out who frequented the Inn and why. A knowledgeable waiter informed us that Hartness was not only once Governor of Vermont in the 1920's, but was also an inventor with hundreds of machinery patents, an astronomer, and an aviator who once crossed the Atlantic in a German Zeppelin. He invented the flat turret lathe and multiple variations thereof, along with a slew of other machinery-related inventions that revolutionized mass manufacturing. He was also into optics and astronomy and invented the revolving dome on an equatorial plane with an interior lens arrangement that precluded an opening for the telescope to emit through.

Back in the 70's through the 90's, Japanese machinist and factory businessmen revered this man and made pilgrimages to the Inn to honor him. Only the male came though, thus only the need for the small motel-like room. The main house rooms were used by members of The National Astronomers Society who paid homage to the observatory on the front lawn and a few B&B diehards who crossed it off their list of Inns to see in Vermont. This was not the romantic property we were looking for and we continued our search.

We continued looking in Vermont from time-to-time and on one trip found a property in a small town operated by two gay gentlemen. We stayed overnight in town to take a second look and, since I was still in Rotary, I attended a meeting to avoid paying a "missed meeting" fine when we returned home. The program at this meeting had to do with wood burning stoves and the number of cords of wood it took to heat a home during a typical Vermont winter. I began having reservations about living in New England about this time.

Nevertheless, we continuing looking up there and visited Inns in Concord, New Hampshire, where winds topped seventy miles per hour on nearby Mount Washington; Stowe, Vermont, where the Von Trapp family (Sound of Music) allegedly relocated to open an Inn; and, in Manchester, Vermont, where I had visited solo to check out a property. After ruling out both properties in Manchester, I was driving out of town on route 7 and drove past a B&B that had great street appeal. I said "what the hell," and turned into their driveway and knocked on the door. A man opened the door slightly and said they were not open for business as yet that day and I blurted out "Are you for sale by any chance?"

The man opened the door fully, took a step out to look around, invited me inside, and closed the door behind us quickly. It turned out the property was for sale unofficially because the wife no longer was interested in operating a B&B and had taken a job in town. The elderly husband still enjoyed the B&B lifestyle but could not operate the property by himself. It only had four bedrooms to offer and another bedroom used by their son. The best part of the structure was reserved for owner's quarters and an additional wing of this 1764 manor house had not yet been restored. I stayed the night in the son's bedroom, as he was away at College, and talked with the husband for quite a while. The wife was not too happy with my presence and was apparently undecided about selling the property.

Sandy and I returned to the property again at a later date and she saw the potential for adding another five or six bedrooms. We decided to make an offer after checking out the town and location. In that area of Vermont, residents were given an option of attending the local public schools or attending a private school on a voucher system. Also, the local municipal budget was voted on annually by residents, and State legislators were non-salaried. There was nothing not to like about living there, except maybe the weather. But even that had a good side, as there was a ski resort nearby that brought in skiers looking for accommodations and Manchester was in the heart of "fall leaf mania". We returned home and did our due diligence on the property, as best we could from long distance.

I found out how much they paid for the property and Sandy analyzed their financials, which told us the wife did not take the job in town because she was just bored. There was not any realtor involved and we negotiated directly with the owners, which might have been a mistake. I returned alone and met with the husband and semi-hostile wife. Our offer was tempered by the need to put a lot of cash into the business to add extra bedrooms, and the husband viewed it as a lowball offer and was offended. The damage was done and he did not return phone calls, or agree to meet again. The "rule of thumb" on valuing an existing up and running Inn, at the time, was four times the gross revenue generated. Our offer was predicated on that formula and not that far out of line, we thought. It turned out that owners always thought their property was worth more than it was, and it took being on the market a while to overcome this mistake. This property had not even been officially on the market yet, so they were not interested in negotiating. I packed up and headed south back to D.C., where Sandy was attending another hospital meeting.

My daydream Inn was the Inn on Golden pond, also in Vermont. Having seen the movie with the Fonda's starring in it, I was elated to find an Inn located on the Pond itself and made some inquiries. My contact was Bambi, the wife of the husband/wife team that had purchased the inn and she graciously shared information about the property they had purchased a year or two earlier. What they had paid for the property, the fact it sat on a road across from the pond itself, and her interest in possibly selling the operation after such a short period of ownership, turned me off and shattered my dream.

We were becoming discouraged after searching for almost two years and concerned that I was not getting any younger. Sandy was getting a lot of pressure at her job to generate a net profit under any circumstances, and it was affecting her health. We were almost to the point of setting a deadline on finding a suitable property or giving up the idea and me finding another job. It was January of 1996 and our B&B clock was ticking. The Country, and California in particular, was beginning to unravel, with the Rodney King riots in L.A., followed by the O.J. Simpson mess, the Oklahoma City bombing, and the World Trade Center basement bombing having occurred over the previous four years. It was now or never for us if the Bed and Breakfast option was to happen.

On the flight out to the hospital meeting in D.C., I had found another Inn for sale in one of the B&B Journals, which was located in Pennsylvania and close to my route from Manchester back to D.C. via highway 81. I diverted ten miles west on highway 16, off of 81, to the small town of Mercersburg and found the Mercersburg Inn, after driving by it on the way into town initially. After a quick walk-through, I drove back to D.C. and told Sandy she had to come back with me and see the property. I must have sounded excited because she decided to forgo the last day of meetings and drive back up to Mercersburg. I cannot say it was love at first sight, but it came close to being what we both wanted in terms of existing amenities and potential to both improve and expand the operation. Other than the castle in Maine, it was the best property we had seen in our two-year active search outside of California.

The Mercersburg Inn was an operating 15 guestroom Country Inn under the Vermont tiled roof of a 20,000 square foot 1909 Colonial Revival Style mansion, situated on five terraced acres on a hill in the small town of Mercersburg, Pennsylvania. It featured a grand entry hall with two curved stairways, stained glass both inside and outside, Tiffany chandeliers, scagliola columns, mahogany and chestnut paneling, decorative tile, white oak flooring with some inlay, and an arts and crafts sun room with a tile floor. It also had a 5000 square foot, two-storied, carriage house with a basement. The Inn had a restaurant and full bar service in two bars, breakfast included in the room rate, a game room with pool table in the basement, and a 2-bedroom owner's quarters, also in the basement. The original hardwood floors were intact on the three floors above the basement. The commercial kitchen was designed to feed 300 and the mahogany paneled dining room and adjoining sun porch sat 60 for dinner. This is what we saw on our original visit and it was enough to get our attention.

We returned home and set about developing an offer that we could afford and not be considerable low ball. The property was listed with a local real estate agent, which indicated the sellers were not very sophisticated and attempting to maximize their gain on investment with a low real estate fee. We found out some valuable information from the agent, who had absolutely no experience in selling commercial real estate, or hospitality property for that matter. The original mansion, called Prospect, was built by a wealthy family in 1909, who occupied it until 1953. It was sold at auction in 1954 and operated as a hotel, with the owners living in the upstairs apartment in the carriage house. In addition to being the birthplace of a U.S. President (James Buchanan), Mercersburg was the home of the Mercersburg Academy, one of the top eight private high schools in America. The current owners of the inn were two young brothers, one just out of college and one attending the Mercersburg Academy across the street, and they were motivated to sell. Their mother/owner had recently died of cancer and their father/former owner had run off a few years earlier with a guest, and left them to run the newly opened Inn.

Historical financial information was obtained and analyzed by Sandy, and a preliminary offer was made and countered. I returned to Mercersburg for negotiations and booked a room at the Inn. I toured the town, the 300-acre Academy directly across the street, and the parts of the Inn Sandy and I had not seen on our initial visit. One evening I was taken out to dinner in nearby Hagerstown, Maryland, by the two brothers and their mentor from the Academy, Jim Smith. The older brother dated Mr. Smith's daughter and Smith sort of kept an eye out for the brother's, although I had a feeling the absentee father was advising them from a distance.

Mr. Smith drove a vintage Cadillac, taught music at the Academy, lived and owned rental property in town, and was the unofficial local historian. He claimed the town was a classic example of a functioning historical town with most everything a business or resident needed to function or live. He was a one-man Chamber of Commerce for the area and the Borough of Mercersburg in particular. The nearby Whitetail Ski Resort, 300-acre Academy, proximity to historical Gettysburg, geographical proximity to Baltimore, D.C., Pittsburg, and even New York City, was covered by his rhetoric during dinner. I was sold on the property by dessert, and only price and terms remained to convince Sandy that the Mercersburg Inn was the right fit for our family. When I left town, we had an agreement in principle, with only terms and our financial position to be checked out by our potential loan vendor, the First National Bank of Mercersburg.

Sandy had met with the bank manager during our first visit to Mercersburg and charmed the socks off him, as she usually did to people. This small-town bank was privately owned and had more in assets than larger banks in the County. You could only buy stock in the bank when a stockholder died and the stock was being sold at auction. The selling price of the Inn was only slightly more than the listing price of our house in California, and our 401k's covered the difference. Plus, Sandy was still working and her six-figure salary and our savings accounts that still held my severance pay and stock sale proceeds from Maxicare were impressive. Our financial situation passed their scrutiny.

Terms proved to be difficult because we wanted to assume a $175,000 note the owners had made with the Borough of Mercersburg. The owners had used the proceeds of the note to make improvements in the Inn and any assumption of the note had to be approved by the City Council for the Borough, and the First National Bank of Mercersburg. Easier said than done, but It did get done! We had befriended the female City Manager (yes, a town of 1476 souls had a City Manager), thanks again to Sandy, who got it past the not too friendly City Council. Sandy came up with pre-paying $25,000 of the note, thus smoothing over some of the Council member's feathers concerning some defaulted payments by the previous owners. We then assumed a $150,000 note with the Borough of Mercersburg.

We also had to negotiate a second mortgage with the owners for $80,000, to keep them engaged with the property until the liquor license could be conveyed from them to us (a very long story, to follow, but first we have to get through the purchase of the Inn.) Buying the Inn turned out to be no different than buying a house, mostly because that was all the real estate agent knew about. The structural inspection was performed by a house inspector, we found out later, who was used to inspecting 700 square foot tract houses. All he found wrong, in 25,000 square feet of 1909 construction and some 1987 remodeling, was exposed wiring in a junction box in the laundry room ceiling and a problem with the recording of the radon gas level in the basement. They were supposed to measure the radon level over a 24-hour period, but because the meter was plugged in to an electrical socket that was controlled by a light switch, the readings were inconclusive. Every night when the lights were turned out the meter was turned off, supposedly. Some of the readings were suspiciously high, but the report could not be validated because it did not cover a 24-hour period. We overlooked this because of the tight time period in closing and because we were anxious to take over the operation and become innkeepers. I worried about radon exposure the whole time we had the Inn, especially since we lived in the basement most of the time we were there. We also discovered many structural problems later on that a commercial building inspector would have discovered. The first of many mistakes we would make going forward.

As things began to come together, we made a questionable decision to take a truckload of furniture from our house in Santa Rosa, California, to the Inn, before the deal closed. We rented a large Penske truck and loaded it with furniture we could utilize at the Inn and in our owner's quarter's. We also rented a car trailer to haul my Jaguar behind the truck. The plan was to drive out, close the deal, unload the furniture; and have me stay to run the Inn and Sandy return to Santa Rosa to sell the house and move her, Megan, and the German Shepherd back to Mercersburg.

Sandy and I left Santa Rosa at night, in a thunderstorm, driving a big truck and towing the Jaguar on a car trailer. Megan went to horse camp in Healdsburg the week we were going to be gone. The cab of the truck had a sliding glass rear window that opened into the enclosed bed of the truck. When loading the furniture, we positioned a sofa facing the rear window, so that one of us could climb back through the window and sleep on the sofa while the other drove. That first night of driving in a torrential downpour, in an unfamiliar truck towing a car trailer that was constantly fishtailing because its wheelbase would get stuck in pavement ruts of eighteen wheelers, was a nightmare. Conditions improved when daylight came and the rain stopped, but the pavement ruts in the slow lane continued on highway 40 all the way across the country. Sandy and I took turns driving and only made one motel stop during the trip.

We made it safely to Mercersburg and closed the deal on May 31, 1996, but not before literally "stumbling" on a potential deal breaker. On the day before closing, I was walking the property looking for the boundary markers and tripped on what I thought was a sprinkler head between the house and street.

There had been no mention of a sprinkler system being present on the five-acre property and I was pleasantly surprised with my discovery. When I mentioned it later to one of the staff, it was news to him, and upon further investigation it turned out to be a fill valve for an old buried furnace oil tank. That raised a flag for our attorney, who became concerned about potential EPA problems with contaminated soil, and the fact it had not been disclosed. The owner's attorney embarrassingly agreed to set aside four thousand dollars in escrow to deal with testing and any subsequent problem "unearthed." The soil did prove to be contaminated and excavation and removal was necessary. It was done at a later date and closing was consummated as scheduled. Two interesting things came out of this occurrence. The amount required to remedy the situation came to $3999, and when I inquired as to what they did with the contaminated soil, the truck driver said they took it down to West Virginia and dumped it.

The day after closing, Sandy, me, and the staff unloaded the truck, and returned it to Penske. Sandy stayed on a couple of days to meet the staff and set up the owner's quarters in the basement, assigning me a few projects to complete before her return with the rest of our furniture,

Megan, and the pets. She also placed the furniture we brought from home strategically throughout the Inn, which essentially began the reorientation of staff to how things were going to be done in the future. Sandy then flew back to Santa Rosa to complete the sale of our house that had magically sold during our three-day absence.

Sandy had a premonition about the sale of our Blackhawk house some five years earlier, when she predicted we would have an offer waiting for us at Silverado Country Club, as we drove over there for a New Year's Eve weekend. We had not had an offer during the whole year it had been on the market. When we checked into our room, the telephone message light was on with a message from our realtor saying we had received an offer, which turned into a sale. It was Sandy that just knew the Inn would close on schedule, and prompted us to load up the truck with furniture and drive back to Mercersburg before we knew the deal would close. On our road trip out in the truck, somewhere in Oklahoma, Sandy announced to me that we would have two offers on our house when we got to the Inn. On our first night, in Room Eight at the Mercersburg Inn, Sandy answered the telephone to hear that we had an offer on our Santa Rosa house.

Selling our house in Santa Rosa had been very problematic and we had tried for almost a year to sell it. Sandy was convinced it did not sell because we had forgotten to dig up the statue of St. Joseph we had buried upside down in front of the mailbox at the Blackhawk house. First, we tried by owner, with just a sign out front because we always had a lot of street traffic due to its great street appeal, and having been on the cover of a real estate magazine. Then California went into one of its eight-year real estate sign wave curves and real estate values in Northern California dropped 25 per cent as it reached the bottom of the curve. I talked to four realtors and all told me we would be lucky to get back what we paid for the house, before real estate fees and closing costs. We needed to come out ahead on this house in order to recoup some of the down payment we made on the Inn. Buying the Inn without having sold our house was not very prudent, but timing was everything as there had been another buyer, allegedly. About this time, one of our neighbors on the cul-de-sac we lived on stopped me when I was walking with Sheba, our Shepherd, and asked if we were having any luck with our sign out front?

They had moved in a year previously, before the real estate market went in the tank, and were an older couple who bought houses, remodeled the kitchens, and flipped the house at a profit. They used a real estate agent who got them the asking price on the last three houses they flipped. The agent did not know much about real estate, but she was one hell of a marketer. We would have to do some of the paperwork, but nothing too complicated. I took the offered agent's card and gave her a call. Sandy and I met with her and, after touring the house, she gave us her marketing plan. She would not market it in Northern California because everyone knew values were down 25 per cent. She would market it in Southern California (another state in her opinion) and other states. She asked what price to list it at and did not blink an eye at our inflated number. Her comment was that "price would not be an issue with this house." When we said time was an issue and gave the reasons why, she said she would take a 30-day listing and work full-time at it. We signed up with her, took down our sign, and left with the truckload of furniture a short time later.

By the time Sandy returned home to Santa Rosa, there were two offers on the house. The best, and winning, offer came from a woman who then lived in Southern California. She used to live in the Santa Rosa area and always wanted to buy our house, but it was too expensive. She would have choked if she knew we had bought it five years earlier for $200,000 under the asking price. She was now willing to pay close to our asking price, which was more than we paid for it, but still less than our asking price. As escrow progressed on our house, Sandy found out, firsthand, how little our marketer/agent knew about real estate. Sandy handed in her resignation from her CFO position at Santa Rosa Memorial Hospital, and began packing up the house for the move back east. It should be mentioned at this time, that Sandy could have declared a "medical stress" disability, upon the advice of her physician, and received 60% of her six-figure salary until age 65, but "Sister Sandy" did not feel this to be appropriate. Before she left Santa Rosa for the Inn, Sandy had all the kids and spouses up for a farewell dinner. She made shrimp scampi, my son's favorite "Sandy Dinner", and he proceeded to devour 21 shrimp. The next day he was hospitalized for an unknown ailment which was never disclosed, but we suspected it was "shrimpitis". I suspect it was drug related.

It was about this time that Megan experienced her paranormal experience in the Santa Rosa house. She had always kept all the lights on upstairs at night, where hers, two other empty bedrooms, and the infamous bloodied game room were located. We had never told her about the true original of the big stain in the middle of the game room carpet, which was there when we moved in, for fear of scaring her. It was only after some time in Mercersburg that we told her and then it only confirmed what she experienced. She claimed to never sleeping very well in that house and would sometimes get up and go down to the family room and watch TV (unknown to Sandy and me.) She was barely thirteen years old and had lived through the Polly Klass thing in nearby Petaluma and a similar crime in Santa Rosa a year later. One night she arose and went into the hallway to go downstairs, but heard something in one of the bedrooms at the opposite end of the hall. She tip-toed down the hall and peaked in the room, thinking it was Sandy, and saw a woman sitting on the edge of the bed with her legs straight out and staring at the mirrored closet doors. Still thinking it was her Mom, she called out and the lady, or vision, disappeared. Megan never told anyone about this for a long time, and still believes it happened. She dismisses any explanation that she dreamed the whole thing by reminding everyone that she never slept much in that house. I was now living in a 1909 mansion with lots of stories and no ghosts that I ran across, but others allegedly had.

INNKEEPERS AT LAST

At fifty-seven years of age, I became an innkeeper, at last; a little bit long-of-tooth to be starting a new career. Sandy was nine years younger, at forty-eight, and closer to the average age for aspiring innkeepers. I tried to stay out of the way of the current staff by simply observing operations for the first few weeks and concentrated on completing projects involving modifications to the owners living quarters in the basement. My first endeavor was to lay laminate hardwood flooring in the hallways and I did this during the day and manned the front desk upstairs during the evening hours. I learned how to close out the books each night on an ancient computer that used equally ancient financial software that was down more than it was up functioning. I also got to know the current staff that was keeping things running during the transition in ownership.

Staff included three full-time innkeepers (including myself), a chef that did dinner for quests on Friday and Saturday nights and special events and weddings and was paid as a full-time employee; and part-time wait staff, kitchen helpers/dishwasher, breakfast help, and a grounds keeper. Housekeeping, maintenance, laundry, and payroll were contracted out. There was a laundry room in the basement with two washing machines and a big dryer that came over on the Mayflower, a separate water heater, and a large table for folding laundry. Bed linens were sent out to the laundry, and towels, table napkins, rags, and other small items were laundered in house. I replaced the former owner and performed a lot of what he did, which turned out to be not much. The operation was on a downward spiral due to owner neglect, lack of advertising/ marketing, and no business plan. The former twenty-two-year-old owner was just keeping the place going until it sold.

It became evident early on that the Inn needed a vehicle to haul laundry, grocery shop, plow snow in the winter, transport guests, and perform any number of tasks that my Jaguar could not do. We decided to buy a new Suburban and set about looking at the local Chevrolet dealer for such a vehicle. When I found a four-wheel drive Suburban that met our criteria, Sandy went down to the dealership in Santa Rosa and drove one to see if she liked such a vehicle. After it passed the "Sandy test," and she chose a color, I purchased a 1996 Suburban from the Chevrolet dealership in Mercersburg, on a Monday. It could not be on a weekend because the dealership closed on weekends. I had gone down there on a Saturday and found it closed and likewise on Sunday. When I inquired on Monday if there was a reason for the dealership being closed these two days, I was told, in no uncertain terms, that most businesses locally were closed on weekends, unlike in California. It turned out that most of the town also closed down on Wednesday afternoons.

I had to wait for a couple of weeks until they could locate a Suburban that had all the bells and whistles we wanted. I was told that dealerships throughout the country were only given one suburban and would have to shop a "special order" with other dealers to find the one they wanted. The one exception was Texas, and Galveston in particular, and that was because they were illegally shipping Suburban's to third world countries, at inflated prices. In the interim period, during which my suburban was being shopped, I invited the local Chamber of Commerce to have their next monthly meeting at the Inn, as a breakfast meeting. They jumped at the chance and we had a standing-room only breakfast buffet with me as the featured program. It went well and I chose to refuse a request from the local newspaper for an interview until Sandy arrived, even though we needed the exposure.

The Suburban finally arrived and I was summoned to go down and sign the paperwork and pick up the vehicle, on a weekday, of course. Upon my arrival, I was informed that I could not lease the car because the bank they used for leasing did not know me, but they would be happy to sell it to me. When I pressed the issue of leasing and the fact that it was a given they would not know me personally, having lived in California the past 36 years, they confided that California was the issue. I called my contact at the local bank, which loaned us the money to buy the Inn, and he said he would provide a loan to purchase the car and to hand the phone to the salesman. Ten minutes later, I drove the new Suburban off the lot and stopped by at the bank. The manager congratulated me on the purchase and said to come back later and sign the loan papers. Later that afternoon, I received a call from the President of the Chamber of Commerce who congratulated me on buying a new Suburban. News travelled fast in Mercersburg.

The Chamber of Commerce did not just represent the town of Mercersburg, or just the county (Franklin), but did serve four other Townships that were contiguous to each other. The former owner of the Inn was not a member of the Chamber, but I succumbed to the full court press the Chamber put on following their breakfast meeting at the Inn, and joined. From past experience during my tenure as a Hospital Administrator, I knew that belonging to community organizations offered access to community leaders, and would be a missed opportunity if I declined. Unfortunately, such was not the case with the Tuscarora Chamber of Commerce. The single purpose of this August body was to collect dues, which were used to fund the annual Townfest. I found out, at my first Chamber meeting, that a majority of those present were not business owners, or even represented a business. They were mostly bored housewives looking for something to do. A couple of us business men attempted to get the Chamber back on course by rewriting the Chamber by-laws, particularly the criteria for membership, but all we accomplished was to piss off some tenured non-business owners who managed to get a new classification for membership in the Chamber, Associate Member.

I managed to stave off joining the other local service groups in town, the Lions, Rotary, and Kiwanis, by saying it would not be prudent to join one without joining all of them, and there was not enough time in the day for me to do so. I could have rejoined Rotary, of which I was a member during my Hospital Administration days, but once they went co-ed back in the 1980's I gave up on that organization. I remained in the Chamber until another opportunity to serve the community came up a couple of years later.

I was a duck out of water when it came to running an Inn and especially a restaurant. The current staff picked up on this right away and knew I could not operate effectively by firing any of them. With the former owner leaving, we were down to two innkeepers, so I was relegated to that function. Sally was the dayshift innkeeper and did the books, staffing, and procurement of supplies. Staffing included scheduling the contracted services for housekeeping, laundry, grounds maintenance, and "other," which included a long list of items. Sally and her husband lived in a structure built into the side of a hill, and partially underground, outside of town. Her and her husband rewove wicker chair seats for a living, in addition to Sally working at the Inn. John was the afternoon/evening innkeeper and did marketing, special events, maître d' for the restaurant, bar manager, and all-around gopher. He lived in town with his ailing mother and had a part-time girlfriend. David was the chef that prepared a four-course pre fixe dinner on Friday and Saturday nights and the food for any special events. These three, and myself, were the only full-time staff when we took over the operation. In addition, there was part time kitchen help, wait staff, and a groundskeeper. A high school girl came in the mornings to set up a continental breakfast consisting of Costco pastries, juice and coffee. I initiated very little change and just "went with the flow," until Sandy got there.

My first project was to prepare the owner's quarters in the basement before Sandy and Megan arrived sometime late that summer. There were two bedrooms, two bathrooms, office, and a large kitchen area that were all in need of a good cleaning and updating. The kitchen area had been converted into a pub by the young former owner after his mother died. It had a separate entrance to the outside and two entrances to the inn upstairs. There was a bar with coolers and bar sinks, tables and chairs, and the mandatory television hanging from the ceiling. I was not about to touch this area until Sandy arrived, as she had already laid claim to the space to become the owner's quarters kitchen. I put down laminated hardwood flooring in the hallways of the apartment, replaced the carpet in both bedrooms and the office, and built a walk-in closet for the master bedroom by walling off part of a hallway. It was not the Ritz Carlton, but it would have to do until we had more money.

At the same time, there were some quick-fix items that needed to be done to the Inn itself. There were some damaged areas on the second-floor hallway hardwood floors and the hardwood floors on the first floor needed to be refinished. This work had to be done by professionals and this was my first taste at hiring local talent. I resorted to the yellow pages and the first of four "floor specialist" showed up two hours late and assured me he could do the job. He went up to the second floor and took out a piece of the flooring which he took with him to go find some matching white oak. He never returned and, after a week of waiting, I moved on to the next guy in the yellow pages. He came a day later than scheduled, but started work immediately with sanding some of the second floor. Once sanding of hardwood floors begins, dust becomes a major issue and there is no turning back. He quit after two days because the dust was aggravating his asthma. When number three arrived, I explained that time was of the essence because my wife was arriving soon with the rest of our furniture. I moved him down to the first floor Rose Room where the baby grand piano would be going when Sandy arrived with it. He lasted half a day before informing me that he just landed a big job up in Harrisburg and had to go where the money was! Third time was not the charm, but my fourth pick was a winner. He showed up, was always on time, and worked hard....a rare combination I was to find out with subsequent projects. The floors were completed prior to Sandy's arrival later that summer, and I ended up selling my 1986 Jaguar to a guest to cover the $6500 expense.

My Jaguar was the topic of conversation at the local Sunoco gas station every time I went down there to gas up. It had dual gas tanks that each held 11 ½ gallons, which could be accessed by use of a switch on the dashboard. This station was a throwback to the 40's and 50's, when an attendant would pump your gas, check the oil, and wash your windshield. Only when I pulled up, everyone came out to see the dual gas caps and debate the need for such a ridiculous arrangement. I would not go anywhere else, however, because the service was unique. If I wanted a vehicle serviced, they would come get the car and return it when finished. When the Jaguar developed a noisy leak in the manifold, I took it to a garage that serviced Jags and they said they would have to remove the engine to get to the manifold, and it would be very expensive. One day when I was getting gas and the usual verbal abuse at the Sunoco station, the owner came out and inquired about the loud noise coming from under the hood. When I explained the manifold problem, he said he could probably weld a patch on the leak and I agreed to let him try. He came up to the Inn to get the car and returned it two hours later without a leaking manifold. He charged me $20 and when I told him that was not enough, he said it was worth it to him to get to work on such a car. I ended up selling the car to a guest who wanted it for his son at college.

During the 50 to 60 days I was at the Inn without Sandy, I never made the transition from want-a-be to an owner. I did not make any significant changes in policy or procedure and felt like one of the staff. I did terminate the grounds keeping position when I found out he was a schoolteacher and cutting our grass on weekends for $15.00 an hour. I learned to navigate the 48-inch Dixon riding mower and mowed the five acres of terraced lawns myself. I also became the maintenance man for the Inn. I learned quickly how to maintain the steam boiler, reverse osmosis water purification system, walk-in freezer, pre-civil war dryer, dish machine, telephone system, antique computer system, ice machine, fire alarm system, and twenty-two toilets, among other things.

In addition to closing down our house in Santa Rosa, terminating her job, and supervising the loading of the moving van, Sandy oversaw the mountain of paperwork associated with transferring ownership of a business. She formed a Sub-Chapter S Corporation to own the assets and lease back the Inn to us, arranged for a Tax ID number, set up the sales tax paperwork, worked with the bank and City Manager on various loans, set up the various insurance coverages, and carried out a million other functions long distance. I did my little projects, worked my shifts, learned some of the back-of-house chores, like shopping and laundry, and read up on the local geography and history.

Walt Filkowski

WHAT PLANET IS MERCERSBURG, PA ON?

The first thing our friends would ask when we told them we had purchased an Inn was where was it, and then, where in hell is Mercersburg, Pennsylvania? It is located in south-central Pennsylvania at the foot of the Tuscarora Mountains seven miles north of the Mason-Dixon Line, the northern border of Maryland. Specifically, it is a Borough in Franklin County, 73 miles southwest of Harrisburg, the capital of Pennsylvania. It comprised about one square mile of land, a population of around 1400, is designated a Historic District, and located on state highway 16 ten miles west of Interstate 81. It was one of the two municipalities in Pennsylvania where the whole town was designated a historic district. A railroad spur ran through the town when the old tannery was operating and students from the Academy would arrive and depart by rail, but it was abandoned in the early 1950's. A pizza restaurant now occupies the old train station.

From a hospitality business standpoint, Mercersburg was located 90 minutes from both Washington D.C. and Baltimore, 2 ½ hours from Pittsburg and Philadelphia, and a drivable 4 ½ hours from New York City. To quote the Inn brochure, "just a picnic basket away from Gettysburg and Antietam battlefields, Harper's Ferry, Berkeley Springs, and Fort Frederick." Mercersburg is surrounded by the rolling green farmlands of picturesque Cumberland Valley, just 10 minutes from Whitetail Ski Resort and the renowned championship golf club, Greencastle Greens."

The village itself was originally called Black town, after its founder, James Black, acquired the land in the middle 1700's from the Indians for a gun and a string of beads. He sold it to William Smith, Sr. in 1759, whose son William Junior laid out the now Smith's Town in 1786. At the suggestion of George Washington, William Junior re-named the town Mercersburg in honor of Hugh Mercer, who served under Washington in the Revolutionary War as a General, came to the area in 1746, and died in the Battle of Princetown in 1777.

Advantageously situated on the main wagon road from Baltimore to Pittsburg (now route 16), Mercersburg quickly became a center for commerce and travel. There was a toll station at the end of town where travelers paid a fee to travel the road. In the early 1800's, Mercersburg became a center for education. In 1836, Marshall College was chartered, but plagued with financial problems it merged with Franklin College in Lancaster, Pennsylvania in 1853. The preparatory division of Marshal College remained in Mercersburg and eventually became known as Mercersburg Academy in 1893. Also, in 1836, The Theological Seminary was established, producing many theologians and the Mercersburg Theology, while affiliated with Marshall College.

All of the foregoing information was made available by the Woman's Club of Mercersburg in the town library that summer, and on Wikipedia as I write this.

Mercersburg actually played a role in the Civil War, in that James Buchanan, fifteenth President of the United States and who was succeeded in the Presidency by Abraham Lincoln, was born and raised here. Many refer to Buchanan as "the do-nothing President," who allegedly "sat on his hands" while the nation drifted towards civil war. Also, story has it that in the weeks preceding the Gettysburg conflict, the Confederate cavalry office and avowed "ladies' man", Jeb Stuart, rode into Mercersburg on a scouting mission and remained several days while being entertained by some local ladies of questionable reputation. Cavalry was the only means of reconnaissance in those days, which may have left General Robert E. Lee blind as to Union Forces whereabouts. A year before we left Mercersburg, the Borough initiated a reenactment of Jeb Stuart's "raid" on the town. His interaction with the ladies was changed to lunch with the wives of Union military men off fighting the war elsewhere, for the sake of schoolchildren.

Reenactments were a big deal in the area with most involving the Civil War, but the French and Indian War, War of 1812, Revolutionary

War and both World Wars were also remembered with small reenactments. The most memorable of the reenactments for us was the first ever reenactment of the Battle of Antietam. The actual battlefield had never been open to the public, but an adjacent farm became available and became the site of Antietam's first ever reenactment. Some of the reenactors stayed at the Inn during the event so we had firsthand knowledge of what occurred during that inaugural reenactment.

The Battle of Antietam was the first major battle of the war fought on Union soil (Maryland was Union at that point) and the bloodiest single day of the entire war. Twenty-three thousand men were killed, wounded, or missing during twelve hours of fighting on that late summer day in 1862. Serious Reenactors everywhere waited years for the opportunity to do their thing at Antietam. Authenticity is the name of the game with these people, even down to the buttons on the uniforms and how they are sewn on. This dedication to authenticity resulted in numerous casualties among the Confederate troop reenactors, who dressed in their woolen winter uniforms on a 90-degree day, as the original southern troops had done, and paid the price with heat stroke. Some even walked barefoot, as their heroes had done because boots and shoes were scarce in the Confederate Army, and paid the price with blisters and lacerated feet. Those on both sides who endured long marches to get to the battlefield dropped like flies when their hearts gave out from overexertion caused by obesity and being out of shape.

Even the spectators experienced hardships! Organizers of the event estimated a total of 20,000 spectators and reenactors and 100,000 showed up. The battlefield and adjacent farm sat at the intersection of Interstate 81 and Interstate 70, and traffic jams were monumental. There was not enough food and water to feed the reenactors, let alone the spectators, and bathroom facilities equaled what both armies found in 1862. Parking was grossly underestimated and added to the traffic problem. The most startling statistic, however, was the number of spectators wounded by cannon fire. The cannons did not fire a projectile or cannonball of any kind, but did ignite their gunpowder. Each morning at dawn started out with a multi-cannon barrage that shook the countryside. Spectators lined up along the battlefield much the same as they do at golf tournaments when Tiger Woods is hitting a shot from the woods. Each spectator sticks his head out a little further to get a better view and gets closer to the line of flight of the golf ball, but in this case they were getting closer to the muzzle velocity of cannons.

The local press chalked the inaugural reenactment of the Battle of Antietam off to inadequate planning and some local residents proclaimed it a bigger disaster than the original battle, but with fewer casualties. The organizers thought it was great and promised a bigger and better one the next year. The State of Pennsylvania claimed it could not compare to the reenactments held at Gettysburg.

Pennsylvania is a long rectangular state similar to Tennessee, but with twice the population, and ranked sixth in that regard. It has Pittsburg in the west and Philadelphia in the East and not much in between. It has the most municipalities of any state in the Union and each one seems to duplicate the bureaucratic structure of the other. There are numerous burgs, boros, villes, and towns or tons, in the southern half of the state and most have a Mayor, City Council, Police and Fire Department, water district, sewer district, and sometimes a City Manager. The municipality on either side would have the same governmental structure with the same or less population. It was explained to me that the southern area was mostly farmland, either feed crops for dairy farming, and farmers are used to individuality and thinking alone, thus doing anything collaboratively was a foreign concept.

Mercersburg turned out to be a classic example of this logic. They had a Mayor, Borough Council, Water District, Sewer District, Two-engine fire department, 1 ½ man police department, and a female City Manager; for a population under 1500 and one square mile of real estate. The Mayor's main duties were to appoint the Chief of Police and to designate when Halloween was to be celebrated. Halloween was an important decision because it also determined when the big Halloween parade would be held. Apparently, one year the Mayor decided Halloween would be celebrated on a weeknight, which fouled up everyone's plans and he was almost impeached. The City Manager ran the Borough and was in constant conflict with the Borough Council. Being female upset the "good old boys" that had run things forever, and her being pushy female made things even worse. The council could not fire her because they had already lost a wrongful termination lawsuit on a previous City Manager, and this one was a female on top of it. The Council eventually forced her out by lowering her salary each year until it was no longer worth it for her to stay on.

The reason for separate Sewer and Water Commissions was unclear, at first, because sewer fees were based on water usage, but the reasons came to light when I was appointed to the Sewer Commission later on. A local fire department was justified by the numerous fires that occurred in and around town because of the ancient structures and numerous barn fires, but the need for a local one-man Police Department was inefficient and probably not too safe. Every little municipality did the same, however, and whenever talk of a county or regional Police Agency came up; the locals would rebel and ask what would happen to good old Larry, our Police Chief. Larry was a piece of work and will be discussed later.

The largest employer in Mercersburg was the Academy, with 400 students and about that same number in faculty, Administration, and maintenance running its 300-acre campus. The local school district was next with its elementary, middle, and high school. Next in line were a small furniture factory and a couple of small machine shops.

To say that the Academy had an impact on the Borough was an understatement. The campus itself abutted the northern edge of town and was across the street from the Inn on the eastern end. Most of the faculty lived in or near town, as did many of the support staff. The Borough's antiquated sewer system probably felt the biggest impact, with kitchen waste, laundry residue, and human waste from feeding and housing 400 students clogging the system. To complicate matters, the

Academy used several wells on their property for water, thus lowering their sewer fee that was based on water usage. The rest of the Borough paid for this inequity with high sewer fees. In addition, over the years the Academy purchased a lot of real estate in and around town. In the event that the real estate was contiguous to Academy property, which most all of it was, by state law it was not subject to property tax. With several churches located within the Borough, property tax was not a major source of revenue for local government.

On the other hand, the Academy was a big draw and local business benefited somewhat, especially food and beverage establishments and lodging facilities; and specifically, The Mercersburg Inn. The other big draw was the Whitetail Ski Resort, and eventual golf course, located on a small mountain several minutes south of the Borough. To a lesser extent, being the birthplace of a United States President, the proximity of Antietam and Gettysburg, and being a historical site brought tourists to the area.

There were four other small Bed and Breakfasts in the immediate area, three in town and one outside of town. The best of the lot was a four-room house in the middle of town owned by a couple named Bates, and I could not resist referring to them as the Bates Motel, from the movie Psycho. None of these could compare to the grandeur and ambience of The Mercersburg Inn, and this was reflected in their much lower room rates.

A portrayal of Mercersburg would not be complete without mentioning the brick house on the "point." The "point" was located on the east end of town where Highway 16 joined a residential road coming in from the south to form a triangle, on which sat a red brick house that was almost a miniature replica of the Mercersburg Inn. It sat just west of the Inn property line and was often thought to be the Inn itself, or associated with it in some way. It was built by a wealthy eccentric old farmer from up near the I-81 area, was never occupied, and had fallen into disrepair. We looked at purchasing it from time-to-time, but the cost of rehabilitating it would have been too much for us.

Walt Filkowski

MERCERSBURG ACADEMY

The Academy played a significant role in our experience at the Inn. As one of the top eight private high schools in the country, it drew a student body from a global perspective as well a national one, with forty states represented during our time in Mercersburg. Conversely, they admitted only two students each year from the town itself, usually on scholarship due to tuition of $39,000 per year for a boarding student and around $15,000 for a day student. All students had to board during their senior year. That led to a clientele of well-healed parents for the Inn that sought fine dining and upscale accommodations, the two things that were headed south when we took over the operation. The Academy's athletic program also brought wealthy parents from the other schools in their league, like the Blair, Hill, Lawrenceville, and Peddie Schools. Al Gore showed up for his son's football game once while he was Vice-President, and suffered some mild abuse from the all-Republican student body, and a loss on the gridiron. He had landed in a helicopter on a near-by farm and drove to the campus in a fleet of "inconspicuous" black Suburban's.

The Academy had produced 54 Olympiads over the years, in addition to countless notables in all fields and two Academy Award winners, Jimmy Stewart and Benicio Del Toro. Jimmy Stewart's experience at the school is a good story. His father owned a small hardware store in Indiana, Pennsylvania and decided his son would attend Mercersburg Academy. He was not admitted, however, and story had it that the father drove Jimmy to the school and dropped him off anyway. At the time, students could pay their tuition by working odd jobs on campus and Stewart was admitted as a working student. He graduated in 1926 after getting his first taste of acting in a student production, and went on to Princeton where he turned his back on a promising architect career in favor of the theatre.

Another feature of the Academy was the magnificent chapel, which was more of a cathedral. The multi-storied spire is a replica of St.

Mary's the Virgin at Oxford, and contains one of 163 traditional carillons in the United States. The carillon now has fifty bronze bells ranging from ten pounds to 3 ½ tons with metal shavings from the Liberty Bell, Old Ironsides, WWI artillery shells, and other historical pieces collected by alumni and friends of the school. The bells are played from a keyboard that requires pounding and footwork while seated on a stool. A one-hour concert is performed every Sunday by the resident or guest carillonneur. The resident carillonneur during our tenure at the Inn was Jim Smith, the former owner's mentor who became a good friend of ours. The chapel was dedicated in 1926 to WWI soldiers from the Academy who died on the battlefield. Another story was that Calvin Coolidge's wife donated monies to the construction of the chapel in memory of their son, Calvin Junior, who died from a foot infection from playing tennis at the Academy when he was sixteen (before penicillin). All is true except he was playing tennis at the White House.

The Chapel hosted an annual Christmas Candlelight Concert of "Handel's Messiah" put on by the Community Chorale, a tri state group of musicians and singers that practiced separately in different locations and came together once a year for this concert. It was always "standing room" only for this magnificent performance.

Walt Filkowski

PROSPECT

The family history of the original owners of the Inn was an interesting one, and added to the overall aura of the subsequent development of the property itself. Harry and Ione Byron dreamed of building an elegant estate following his assumption of the family tanning business in 1901. His father had moved the tanning business down to Williamsport, Maryland, from upstate New York and Massachusetts in the late 1800s, allegedly because of the proliferation of the type of tree that produced the bark needed to tan leather. They opened a second tannery in Mercersburg in 1895 that specialized in "fancy leather", and Harry was put in charge of it. Harry and Ione found a six-and one-half acre site for their estate on the tallest hill in Mercersburg, and commenced construction after moving an existing house to the southern portion of the property. Named "Prospect", the 20,000 square foot brick mansion was completed in 1909/1910 and was occupied by the Byron family until 1953. The house boasted forty closets at a time when closets were taxed heavily as rooms and only the wealthy could afford them, and was the first house to have electricity in Franklin County.

Situated on a hill overlooking the town and the adjacent Mercersburg Academy, Prospect was located far enough away from the tannery to escape the foul odors emitted from the tanning process, but close enough to run power lines from the tannery up to the house. At the time, electricity was only allowed in a business establishment and not deemed safe for a residence. Apparently, an exception was made for the largest employer in town, with his fairly innovative knob and tube wiring and marble and copper fuse panels. Harry also had to agree not to sell electricity to anyone else in town. There was a duck pin bowling alley in the basement during the Byron residency along with a large walk-in safe with combination lock tumblers.

The brick tri-level carriage house was added shortly after the mansion was completed, and the original house, moved to the rear of the property, was sold off, along with an acre of land, after the estate was sold at auction in 1954. The estate was sold again in 1978, and in 1986 to the people we purchased it from. Extensive rehab and remodeling took place before it was opened again in 1989 as The Mercersburg Inn.

Walt Filkowski

A FAMILY AGAIN

It seemed much longer than the 60 days I was at the Inn without Sandy and Megan. In early July of 1996, Sandy put Megan on a plane with her cat, Mittens, and drove out to Mercersburg with her parents and Sheba, our German shepherd, in her parent's minivan. I picked Megan up at Washington Dulles Airport in Virginia, only a one-hour drive away, and four days later the Thompson clan arrived. I was up in one of the guest rooms taking a nap because carpet was being installed in our basement apartment and I had been up late the night before babysitting a businessman guest. When Sandy came up to wake me up, I guess I did not respond in the manner she thought I should have and this incident has been brought to my attention on numerous occasions since.

Sandy was already upset that an article had appeared in the local and Hagerstown newspapers about a California man buying the Mercersburg Inn. I had assured her that I would not grant an interview with the reporter until we could do it together, but the reporter jumped the gun and used comments I had made at the Chamber of Commerce Inn breakfast to make it appear to be an interview. Things went downhill from there! Sandy hit the ground running and wanted to make some instant changes in the operation and could not understand why I had not already implemented some changes myself. I had been a "change agent" during most of my "black hat" working career in hospital administration and she could not understand why I had not applied this management philosophy during my two months at the Inn.

She would not buy my rationale that I chose not to make a lot of changes because I did not want to risk losing some, or all, of the staff and be left running the Inn by myself. When I continued to resist some of the changes she wanted to make for the same reason, things got tense. She viewed it, in retrospect, as the California man running his Inn the way he wanted to. It all worked out eventually and we did end up losing all three of the full-time staff, but not before we both had a better handle on running things.

One of our early disagreements was the need for our own kitchen in the owner's quarters in the basement. I felt the money would be better spent on improvements on the Inn itself, in view of the large kitchen upstairs, but Sandy prevailed with her argument for her own kitchen that Megan could also use it. The first of many disagreements I would lose. The area she chose for the kitchen was the newly created beer bar designed by the older brother to meet his and his friend's needs. With that priority addressed, Sandy turned her attention to getting Megan enrolled in eighth grade at the local middle school.

This would be Megan's first experience with a public school environment, and a rural public school to boot. She had been in private religious school systems from preschool through seventh grade even though her three older siblings had survived the public school systems in California before her. Unfortunately, she had to ride a school bus for the first time, and this proved to be a less than desirable experience. Megan had to be at the end of our parking lot driveway at 6:30 in the morning to be picked up and then ride throughout the countryside for ninety minutes while the rural farm kids were harvested and taken to school along with her. Eventually we worked it out where I would take her to school and pick her up in the afternoon. She adjusted to the public school environment, made some friends, and announced to the world that she would never go to the Academy with those stuck-up rich kids, the prevailing attitude of the public middle school student population.

Megan did well in her new school environment, and had a good experience in Chemistry, of all subjects. She liked the teacher well enough to go back and visit him a year later. My all-time story about her experience in that middle school (and later told many times to guests) was when local businesspersons were invited to talk to her class about their vocation. A local man who collected, and sold, antique bottles did his presentation, and when asked where he found these old bottles and jars, he responded that he found most of them in outhouses and privies. He would don a rubber wetsuit and mask and jump into these old outdoor repositories of human waste, of which there were still many in use in the local rural environ. He said that in the old days, when drinking was frowned upon and sometimes illegal, the men would retreat to the outhouse to take a swig or two and drop the empty bottle down the hole.

October of our first year rolled around and we got to experience our first Mercersburg Halloween Parade down Highway 16 in front of the Inn, and on into town. From past experience of small town parades, we expected the high school band, fire truck, ambulance and cars full of local politicians. Megan asked to attend with some of her new school friends, and we reluctantly agreed when remembering the California situation. We decided to let her go, but followed along discreetly behind her group of friends. We were treated to a two-hour parade of multiple large bands, floats, clowns, and whatever. The bands competed for prize money which they used for uniforms and transportation costs, and came from miles around. Highway 16 was closed down for the duration of the parade, which must have made the truckers unhappy, and the parade attendees were mostly families, without any teenagers running around loose. The parade extended beyond the eight o'clock weekday curfew for under-eighteen-year old's, and that must have taken an act of congress. It was good to have the trials and tribulations of family life back in my day-to-day existence once again.

THE FIRST MAJOR CRISIS

The first major economic crisis erupted before closing, but had an immediate impact on operations from day one of our ownership. Critical to the cash flow of any restaurant and/or special event business is the sale of alcohol, and to sell alcohol in Pennsylvania required a state liquor license. Pennsylvania at the time was a liquor control state in which the state conducted all business related to alcohol. The state purchased, warehoused, distributed, and sold beer, wine and liquor, and operated their own liquor stores that were staffed by unionized civil servants. Only a limited number of licenses were issue in any one geographical area and it was not uncommon for an establishment to sell their license to another local entity. Transferring a license to a new owner was not a problem except for the cumbersome procedure and paperwork.

It was only a problem if the new owner was from out-of-state and a bigger problem if the new owner was from California. We began the process in April of 1996 while still living in California, with the assistance of a Pennsylvania attorney experienced in such matters. The state was divided into liquor control regions with a bureaucrat of questionable intelligence placed in charge to monitor compliance of liquor laws and perform other administrative duties, such as license transfers. They operated independently "out in the field" and the first step in a transfer involved a site visit to the location of the transfer. Our attorney contacted the state by filing the necessary paperwork and he awaited the site visit, as our representative. After ten days of no activity, he contacted the state and found out the field rep was missing and an all-points bulletin had been issued to help find her. Another week passed and our attorney was notified that the field rep was located after having taken a three-week vacation without telling anyone.

The now rested field rep finally showed up and presented the attorney with a placard announcing the intention of transferring the license that was to be placed in a front window of the establishment facing the most travelled road abutting the building. The fact the location of the 8 by 12 placard would be 50 yards up a hill from highway 16 and unreadable from the inside of the building escaped the keen observation skills of the field rep. She did remind the attorney that the placard had to remain in place for 30 days, which put us past closing and would subsequently require a special arrangement with the previous owner. With that initial step out of the way, we could now proceed with the remaining steps of the process. By this time closing had occurred and I was now the point person since I was on site. Our attorney allegedly knew someone in the liquor control bureaucracy up in the state capitol and could expedite things.

Expedience was the name of the game because we had a large wedding coming up and alcohol was included in the package pricing. The next step was a background check of the new owner, me! My name was on the documents so they wanted to know if I was a felon or all-a-round bad guy. I said no and they said prove it. They wanted proof from the place I lived for five years before coming to PA. Not a problem and I called Sandy in Santa Rosa and asked her to go down to the police station and have them state that I had no arrests or convictions in the past five years. She called back and said they would fax that information to them, but would charge them for the fax. Another week passed without hearing from Harrisburg, which prompted another phone call from our attorney. Their response was they do not accept fax as a legal document. This in turn became an attorney's dream and he began documenting to the state the legal position that some higher court had declared a fax to be a legal document.

By now Sandy had arrived on site and our limited arrangement with the previous owner to carry the liquor license had expired. The large wedding at the Inn was upon us and we agonized over whether or not to charge for the alcohol without a liquor license or to eat the cost. We ended up eating the cost and moving on. A few weeks later, our attorney prevailed and the state said they would accept the fax as a legal document, but they had no provision for paying for the fax and, therefore, could not accept it. I offered to pay the ridiculously small sum, but they said the applicant could not incur any cost for a transfer. By this time our attorney was tearing his hair out and we wondered if there was not a concerted effort to prevent us from getting a liquor license.

I called the next day to find out what I needed to do to expedite the background check and was told not to worry because they had waived it due to not having any provision to pay for the fax. We had wasted weeks on the fax issue and had to eat the cost of alcohol for the wedding and other guest and dinner business, but I had to bite my tongue and thank the lady on the other end of the phone. A week later I opened a letter from the liquor board that congratulated me on obtaining the enclosed liquor license, with no other explanation. With our liquor license in hand, I could now go down to our local state owned liquor store in town and purchased inventory without having to go out of state. This made our new friend from the chapel, Jim Smith, happy because the state rented space in the building he owned for their liquor store. Apparently, the store was not doing well financially and I soon found out why.

The woman running the store not only had no interest in running a business, she also did not know a thing about liquor and specifically about wine. There was not a great wine selection to choose from and the three restaurants in town, including us, could not get her to stock what we wanted. Whenever we complained to Jim Smith about the store manager's ineptness and consequence of the State closing the store, he reminded us of her being civil service and union and unable to be fired. There was a silver lining to this cloud, however, which only The Mercersburg Inn benefited from. I revised our wine list to not only include more upscale wines, but to include the vintage, or date. This had no effect on local consumption, but appealed to the Academy parents who were more knowledgeable when it came to wine. Every once in a while, the local liquor store would purge "old stock" and place "old" red wines on sale to get them off the shelf. I would take all she had to sell, at prices below current vintage of the same wine.

Walt Filkowski

THE FIRST MAJOR MISTAKE

Having sunk all of our liquid assets in the Inn, incurred a sizeable mortgage, and "hitching our wagon to a star," we proceeded to make one of the dumbest moves possible. As fall of 1996 approached, and we had been in business all of four months, Thanksgiving was coming and Sandy's parents were celebrating their 50th wedding anniversary about the same time in Santa Maria, California. Sandy decided the three of us needed to go back to California for both events as her mother's health was failing and it might be the last opportunity to do so. The dilemma was that the Inn was struggling financially and we had spent a bunch already on improvements, so that closing down for a week or more did not seem prudent. One afternoon I took a call from a lady who wanted to know if we would rent the Inn for the week of Thanksgiving to them to hold their annual family retreat.

They usually rented two or three houses close together in some resort area somewhere, but the families were getting so big that now three or more houses were required and they really all wanted to be under one roof. They did not want any Inn staff present as they would cook all their own meals and bring their own food and spirits. They could not give us any references as this would be their first time under one roof, but promised that we would find the Inn in the same condition as we left it. Needless to say, Sandy and I agonized over this proposal, and finally decided it would be the only way we could financially justify going to California. We did insist on having a staff member orient them to the property and to have a staff member on call in case of an emergency. We also set a limit on the number of guests at 40, which were what the guest rooms could sleep, including cots.

It was on the plane heading to California that Sandy and I looked at each other and said "what have we done." We had spent Thanksgiving at her parents in the central coast town of Santa Maria every year since we first dated in 1980, but this year proved to be the most traumatic. Sandy called back to our designated staff person almost daily to find out if they had burned down the place or were having wild parties. It was not all trauma, however, as we had all the extended families under our own "one roof" for Thanksgiving dinner. Megan got to see her sisters Lauri and Dana, along with some uncles, aunts, and cousins; and Sandy spent some time with her mother, which would prove to be for the last time.

When we returned to Mercersburg, we found the Inn as promised, just like we left it only better. The renters loved the place and wanted to reserve it for the next Thanksgiving period, but we had already decided never to do it again. They enjoyed all being under one roof and being in a turn-of-the-century mansion, and the banging steam radiators reminded some of the older family members of time past when this was an every morning experience. We had forgotten to tell them about the steam pipes, as we had only experienced it once or twice before when the heat came on, as we got into the fall months. Living in the basement gave us first-hand knowledge of the deafening noise when the hot steam hit the cold water that had collected in the lower-level pipes after the heat went off the night before. I eventually learned how to drain off the collected water in the morning before the steam boiler kicked into action, and it became just another of my winter "Inn Chores". Sometimes I would be too late, or I just forget to do it, and the guests would either loved it or hate it.

We settled back into running the Inn and prepared for our first Christmas as innkeepers. Changes in the operation were coming hot and heavy now as Sandy began to wrest away my perceived "control" of how things were done. The "institutional" ambiance was replaced with a more "homey" atmosphere and dinner was expanded to three nights by added Thursday, and eventually Sunday was added. The menu was expanded to include a choice of three entrees to the prix fixe instead of the single entrée, and later on an ala carte menu was added. Our "inherited" chef wanted more money now that he was almost working full time, and took the opportunity to quit over a dispute of not being granted vacation with pay before having worked enough hours to have earned it.

We took that opportunity to hire a CIA (Culinary Institute of America) trained chef as we had been advised to do at a seminar. After a couple of years, when faced with hiring our third chef, Sandy used a technique she learned somewhere of having candidates cook a gourmet meat from whatever they found in the Kitchen.

Sandy was doing breakfast, by this time, and was assisted by a former employee who returned when she learned there were new owners, and the high school girl, who came in during the week before school and on weekends. We got to know this young girl quite well and, when we found out she had an interest in physical therapy, related my experience as a therapist to her and encouraged her to pursue this career and get out of Mercersburg. Her mother had come from a long line of young girls in town who got pregnant and abandoned by the father. She seemed excited by the prospect of completing her high school education and moving on to junior college. A few months later she announced she had moved in with her boyfriend and dropped out of school.

We employed another high school girl from nearby McConnellsburg, who was tall and very attractive. She played volleyball in high school and was good enough to get a full scholarship to Shippensburg State College. She lasted one semester in college before returning home to move in with her boyfriend. It was impossible to get these young girls out of this small-town environment.

One of the more pleasant chores that needed to be done at the Inn was purchasing period pieces of furniture to replace a lot of the garage sale pieces that we inherited with the purchase of the property. There was an abundance of antique shops in the surrounding area, but we seemed to frequent one in particular that was located ten miles to the east in the little town of Greencastle. We purchased a lot of items there over the years, and even had brief thoughts of purchasing the store when the owner announced she would be retiring. I always had to be restrained on these outings because I thought we were spending "Inn Money" and Sandy would always have to remind me that in the final analysis, it was really our money.

There was not a lot of available cash around in the early days of inn keeping, and what became available was quickly spent on upgrading the operation. Sandy had a thing for Yves Delorme linens and Christy towels and every one of the fifteen guest's rooms were outfitted with 400 count sheets, featherbeds, comforters, wool blankets, and Christy bath sheet towels. We ran across a rug dealer that would rent us quality oriental and Persian rugs for the rooms that we would end up owning over time. There was no end to what we could spend on upgrades, but that was the fun in having the Inn. During that first year, we began upgrades as cash flow allowed. We paved over the cracked and crumbling cement driveways and parking lot, installed a rock driveway completely around the building, thus making the front entrance available from the rear of the property. A well was sunk some 200 feet through slate infested soil to provide irrigation for the five acres, and a French drain was installed in front of the Inn to prevent flooding that occurred in the basement during heavy rains. The two huge thirty-foot columns on the front steps were repaired and painted, but the $30,000 bid to repaint the entire, mostly brick, Inn was ignored. We had to have the limbs on two huge oak trees between the carriage house and the Inn cabled to prevent them from snapping off during periods of heavy snow. The last major project of restoring the sunken gardens was started, but never finished due to my heart episodes. We were actually living in, and enjoying, all the improvements we were making.

We did not need a lot of money to live on. In the eight years we owned the Inn, we never had to pay income tax because we never made a profit, after depreciation. Our only out-of-pocket expense was dry cleaning of our personal items, entertainment, Megan's tuition, non-business travel, and food when we ate out. We estimated that our insurance expense, automobile, household, utilities, and other expense for the three of us totaled about $50,000 a year, and were paid for by the Inn. The IRS actually had a provision to allow this if the Innkeeper lived on the premises. That is how all those 400 little four-room bed and breakfast places made it in Vermont.

Walt Filkowski

VISITORS

Two types of visitors came to see us at the Inn; family and friends, and other. The other category included regulatory agents from the various governmental agencies, i.e., licensing, liquor control, public health, law enforcement, and public works, salespersons, vendors, contractors, and freeloaders. We knew how to deal with the other category from running hospitals, which were the most regulated business in the country.

My first family visitor came while I was at the Inn BS, before Sandy. My oldest sister and her husband drove down from Milford, Pennsylvania, uninvited and unappreciated. I was trying to learn the business, pulling a shift, and not familiar enough with the surrounding area to be much of a tour guide. I was still in the employee/owner dilemma and did not even comp their room when they left. Sandy's parents drove her out here later that summer and stayed a while, and after Sandy had been here a month or two, Dana and her husband came out to visit. Dana had finished law school in May and was studying for the Bar Exam at the time. This was followed by a visit from Lauri, her husband, and their 15 month old son, who were considering moving out to Georgia from California. Scott had already relocated to Seattle from Santa Rosa once he lost access to Sandy's cooking when she left for Mercersburg. We found out later that he ran off to Seattle to escape conviction on a DUI charge.

The following year, in 1997, we had visits from numerous California friends, seven couples along with two of the nuns we had worked with at St. Rose Hospital. After that flurry of activity, we had very few, if any, friends from California come to visit us at the Inn. We, in turn, made several trips back out to California to visit friends and family over the next few years. We had decided from the very beginning that we would always close the Inn for Christmas, mostly for Megan's benefit, but also to give Sandy and me a short break. The second Christmas we invited my two east coast sisters' down from the north, and they, in turn, asked if some of their children and grandchildren could come. In all, we sat twelve for Christmas dinner in the dining room in front of a roaring fire and enjoyed four days of "family." We did that again the following Christmas, but after that we spent Christmas in Peachtree City, Georgia where Lauri and her family had moved to.

Scott moved out from Seattle in 1997 to "help us run the Inn," but neither Sandy nor I remember asking for his help. He sold his van in Seattle and hopped on a train to Baltimore, where I picked him up. I had bought him a used small pick-up truck which he was to reimburse me for, but he informed me he had spent all the proceeds from selling his van on food during his three-day train trip. I suspected he had spent it on beer mostly, but we chalked it up to Scott being Scott. Without any money, he had to be housed at the Inn, and we put him to work doing maintenance jobs for the summer until he paid off the truck. We were determined to not allow him to leach off us again, and support himself for once in his life. When the truck was paid off, we told him he would have to pay room and board and he decided to move out and share an apartment with our new chef. At that point, our beer inventory magically stabilized and expense for that line item returned to prior levels.

Scott found a job in one of the small machine shops that were always opening and closing in the area. They would close down as soon as the Wage and Hour people would come to investigate a complaint, only to reopen at another location under a different name. Scott worked a forty-hour night shift without benefits, shift differential, or overtime pay. He had to buy the tools required for the job from the company and paid for them through a payroll deduction, after taxes. Any rags he used on the job had to be purchased from the company also. Unions would have had a field day in this environment. He seemed to enjoy the work, however, and entertained us with on-the-job stories. I took him to play golf one day and when he told his supervisor about it, the man just could not believe anyone could be that stupid to hit and chase a little white ball around a field. Scott was a reader and read whenever he got a chance. One night while on a break, he was reading a book when his supervisor inquired what he was doing. When told he was reading a book, the supervisor when ballistic. Scott said it was like hitting him upside the head with a two-by-four. The supervisor yelled out that Scott not only played golf, but read books as well, and nobody in their right mind did that!

Scott was a smoker and, when not reading on his breaks, would be outside smoking. The parking lot was always full of pick-up trucks with gun racks hanging in the rear window displaying their favorite weapons. Once a month, he would come back into the break room from the parking lot and announce that he had just seen the biggest deer in his life with a huge rack, and stand aside as the room emptied and the men ran to their trucks to retrieve weapons. He claimed to have done this on numerous occasions and they never caught on that he was pulling their chain.

Scott was a good looking young man and had no trouble attracting the ladies. My fear was that he would get one pregnant and take off, as was the local custom. He began dating a really nice girl from a nearby town who had a good job and was interested in furthering her education. He brought her to the Inn a few times and we really hoped their relationship would flourish, but Scott was Scott and it was not to be. I thought that he really did not get over the Danville incident when the father of the girl he really liked ran him off as a loser, and he chose never to get in a serious relationship again. Scott claimed the girl got pregnant and he offered to marry her, but she did not want children to interfere with her going to college. In any event he up and returned to California when his prosecutor sister said she would have to prosecute his DUI, but would help him get started again.

After Sandy's mother died, her father would come out from California each year and spend some time with us. One year, when he was in his late seventies, he struck up an acquaintance with a lady in her sixties that blossomed into a teenage infatuation and then a full blown romance; at least on his part. They had dinner together at the Inn, and afterwards we could hear them scurry along the upstairs hall to each other's rooms. They arranged to be at the Inn at the same time in future years, and he even came back to visit her at her home up in New England, on one occasion. While back in California, he would get up at 4:30 in the morning to call her before she left for work at 7:30 Eastern time. He had a huge cell phone bill every month, and would also send her jewelry, which became a concern of ours. The romance was put on hold when we sold the Inn, but reignited later.

So much for family and friends that visited us at the Inn. Some of the "other classification" visitors are worth mentioning. The most persistent unwanted regulatory visitor was the kitchen public health inspector. He was a short ex-marine, crew-cut hair and all, with a little man complex and a chip on his shoulder. He delighted in showing up unannounced and at the most inconvenient times. He drove a small red car that alerted us when he was on site and gave us a few minutes to straighten up the kitchen.

I had dealt with his kind in my hospital days and knew how to handle him. My initial volley was to disarm him with a request for his advice on how to handle a vexing kitchen problem. This was followed by sharing military war stories from my days in the Navy as we walked around the kitchen and down to the walk-in refrigerator. The Marine/Navy connection seemed to work for some reason even though one branch detested the other while we were active. In most cases, we would arrive back at our starting point with nothing written down on his clipboard. His favorite items in the kitchen to ding you on were the ice machine and the dish washer. Usually, he would make some comment on one or the other as I walked him out the kitchen door, just to let me know we had not gotten off Scott-free. He would leave us and go on downtown to inspect the other restaurants. Our main dinner competitor in town was owned by a Romanian man and his American wife. He was the chef and had a nasty temper that could often be tested by his kitchen and wait staff. Our friendly kitchen inspector was not immune to his temper tantrums, which would result in pages of citations. Of course, I was not above mentioning to the inspector a problem or two I had observed in that establishment to prime him for his visit there.

Other than a benign visit from our liquor control missing lady, the only other notable inspection came from the State Public Works Division, and it involved our low-pressure boiler. The regulations said that only high-pressure boilers came under the jurisdiction of the state, but this gentleman claimed the regulations had been changed to now include low-pressure boilers. I always wondered how they even knew we had a boiler and suspected that a disgruntled terminated contractor had informed them. In any event, violations were discovered and remedies expected in a very short time frame. I was able to fix all of the problems myself, and when the inspector returned, he found only one item that needed to be redone. The state required that the dump valve for escaping excess steam be vented to the outside and I had run the three-inch pipe through the transom over the door leading out of the boiler room to a flight of stairs going up to the ground level outside. On the end of this pipe, I installed a 90 degree fitting that pointed up toward the sky. The inspector wanted the fitting pointed down into the stairwell to eliminate the possibility of anyone walking by to be steam-burned. Of course, anyone exiting that door to escape a potential boiler explosion would be crispy-crittered, but I turned the fitting around and he signed off. I turned it back up after he left!

Two law enforcement visitors come to mind with positive results worth mentioning. The first involved the local Fire Chief and it concerned three of our seven fireplaces in the Inn. Three of our guest rooms had wood-burning fire places and, after our first winter as Innkeepers, I decided to replace these with gas logs. The reason for this change was the frequent call for more wood in the middle of the night. Two of the bedrooms had balconies and additional wood was placed there in addition to an ample supply inside. When I would remind the guest of the wood just outside the balcony door, the reply would be "I am not going out there (in the rain, snow, or cold)". So, I would have to go out there (in the rain, snow, or cold), get the wood, and bring it up to the room. The dining room also had a wood burning fireplace and, while romantic, it was a pain to be constantly stoking or putting more wood on the fire. It was also disturbing to the dinner guests when a gust of wind would back up smoke into the dining room. The game room in the basement also had a fireplace and I decided to install gas logs down there for the convenience of the guests.

So, I began the process of looking into installing gas logs and had a vendor come to recommend size and type. The vendor informed me that because of the age of the building and the fireplace all-brick flues, I would have to line the flues with stainless steel tubing. When I reminded him that people had been burning fires in these fireplaces since 1909 without a problem, and that gas logs did not produce hot embers, he quoted some fire marshal regulations that required stainless steel tubing. Upon review of the regulations, I found the key word always buried somewhere in unreasonable regulations, that word being "unless." In this case, "unless" was followed with …".the local Fire Chief deems it not necessary to do so". Up to the Inn came the local Fire Chief and, in his wisdom and professional opinion, the brick flues in all the chimneys were in excellent condition and stainless-steel tubing was not needed. Case closed! Installation of the gas logs is another story to come later.

Before Sandy arrived on the scene and I had taken on the five-acre grass cutting duties, the local Police Chief paid me a visit. He wanted to know if I would hire a local kid that needed some direction and a job for the summer. I reluctantly agreed, thinking it might be a good idea to cement relations with the local police department. It turned out that the "department" consisted of Chief Larry and a part time assistant Chief. Too many Chief's and not enough Indians came to mind. But things turned out alright and, after some training on the Dixon 48-inch riding mower, the teenager did fine. About three weeks later, we hit a wet spell and it rained a lot. On a day our teenager was supposed to cut the grass, it rained hard and I wanted to call and tell him not to come in, but I did not have his telephone number. I grabbed the local small telephone directory to look up his number while I was sitting on the throne (I could still multi-task). Apparently, his last name was very common because there were at least two hundred of them listed. Later, when his surname appeared in the local paper for a serious crime, I asked him if this was one of his relatives and he shrugged and said it could be, but he had so many he could not keep track. I later learned that the local custom was to have periodic "reunions" of these numerous relatives, at a picnic or other social gathering, at which family trees were explored. Such gatherings were published in the local paper, with instructions on what food or drink items to bring according to where you fell alphabetically.

An unexpected pair of visitors paid us a visit during our second year of operation that could be classified as a "sales call". The husband-and-wife owners of a large Inn and restaurant up in the Pennsylvania Poconos Mountain area showed up one day and announced they were here to evaluate us for membership in "Select Registry, Distinguished Inns of North America". Select Registry is a nonprofit association of independent innkeepers united by a commitment to gracious hospitality and exceptional settings and amenities. Only about 400 of the overall thousands of "inns" and "B&B's" qualify to become members and these must conform to a strict Quality Assurance Program that provides for unannounced periodic quality assurance inspections. Membership proved very expensive, but their marketing program, in the form of an association guidebook, turned out to be our largest source of guests going forward from our acceptance in 1998.

Another "sales" visit turned out to be beneficial when the owner of a large rug dealership came to make us a proposal to rent expensive rugs for our guestrooms instead of buying them outright. We had purchased a large expensive rug from him for our premier guest room, and had indicated our intent to buy more over time when money allowed. He now proposed a rent-to-own program where he would provide quality rugs for all or part of our remaining quest rooms for a fixed monthly price. The rental fee would apply to a purchase price if we decided to buy a particular rug, and we also had the ability to change out rugs at any time. This allowed us to instantly upgrade the rooms and justified raising room rates.

We also began to have drop-in visitors that came just to see a functioning 1909 mansion. We hated to discourage this because such a visit could turn into an overnight or weekend stay or a dinner, but it also meant taking the time to walk someone around or explain some architectural feature. We thought we had a solution to this problem when the Chamber of Commerce asked if we would do an open house type event in conjunction with their annual downtown Christmas bazaar in 1997. The idea was to pick a mid-week day when we could anticipate no guests present and open up the entire Inn, including guest rooms, to the ticket buying masses. We thought by doing so we could slow down the number of looky loo visits and agreed to do it. The Chamber agreed to provide members to act as docents and lead groups of people through various parts of the Inn and the guest rooms. We were also urged to provide some limited refreshments as an inducement to buy the Chamber's tickets. Cookies and lemonade were suggested and advertised in the local papers.

The tour date was upon on us and Sandy, of all people, was not around to host the event. Her mother had died unexpectedly and she had flown back to California for the services. The first thing to go wrong was that only two Chamber members showed up to work, and they had to handle tickets and refreshments. The rest showed up later as visitors to mainly eat the cookies and drink the lemonade. The Chamber had estimated a low turnout because of other events happening downtown at the bazaar, but the bazaar was not offering free cookies and lemonade. We were swamped early on and ran out of the refreshments early, with no one around (like Sandy) to replenish the supply. Refreshments were what they wanted first, and a tour could come later, if there was time. A lot of visitors left after gorging themselves without even stepping out of the refreshment room. Those that arrived after the refreshments ran out, left in a huff and grumbling about the cheap innkeepers. The major issue did not surface until much later when our housekeepers went up to the guest rooms to tidy up and found that beds had been laid on and toilets used and not flushed. Needless to say, that was the first, and last, open house.

Some of our vendors became friends and a few of them come to mind. Our chefs used goat cheese quite a bit and Sandy liked to use it in her own kitchen and in a breakfast entrée item, but it was expensive and not always good quality. A former chef at the Inn had left when the two sons took over and started raising goats on a farm outside of town, with the intent of producing goat cheese to sell commercially. He had spent years developing his operation and had finally passed a very rigorous licensing inspection that would allow him to begin producing and selling goat cheese. He invited us out to tour his facility and we drove out one day to see it. It had rained the night before and his farm was a muddy mess containing several run-down buildings, and a bunch of dirty looking goats. We both wondered how in the world this guy ever got licensed with the mess the farm was in. We came around a run-down old barn and there stood a glistening stainless-steel building that was as immaculate inside as it was on the exterior.

Another "friendly" vendor did our laundry. We sent out bed linens, dinner napkins, tablecloths and some other minor items. Towels, washcloths, and rags were done in-house. When I first arrived at the Inn everything was sent out to a large commercial laundry. They would come pick it up and deliver it back, but not everything always came back. It was getting pricey and the quality was not that good so I paid a visit to their operation in Hagerstown, Maryland, and came away less than enthused. They operated out of an old warehouse with dirt floors and batched loads of laundry from different facilities. Hagerstown was about thirty minutes away and the closest large town that could support a commercial laundry and this laundry was the largest.

The second largest was quite a bit smaller and did not pick-up outside the city limits. It was pretty run down but the owner/operator talked a good game. By this time, Sandy had upgraded all the bed linens and towels and did not want her new inventory destroyed by a seat-of-the-pants laundry or lost in a batching process. We tried him out with good results and I added him to my weekly run to Costco/Sams. If we had a full house weekend or mid-week conference, he would always squeeze us in, and if he was backed up and we were slow I would adjust my pick-up time. It was a good working relationship, which I found to be essential in a small-business operation. The owner was an avid golfer and we would swap golf-lies on my visits, even though I rarely got out playing in those days.

Sandy had her favorite vendors also, but then she could charm a snake out of its skin and had a good working relationship with everyone, except me! She would not allow dancing on the almost one hundred year old reconditioned wood floors, so a portable dance floor had to be rented and set up, either in the great room, or the equally large sun room. As the wedding business grew, the need for outside tenting materialized and the same company that provided the dance floors always responded favorably to her creative tenting needs. The same man seemed to have our account and he and Sandy hit it off famously. Again, a good working relationship helped us out in a lot of light situations.

When Sandy evicted my bar out of the glassed-in Sanitarium to start her gift shop, she established relationships with various vendors that enabled her to purchase volume-restricted items for resale. If a volume-restricted (had to purchase a certain number to get a discount) variance could not be obtained, she would joint-ventured with another Inn to meet the numbers. Over time, she replaced all the mattresses with a Serta special hotel grade mattress and topped it with a featherbed and upgraded bed lines, all of which she sold in her gift shop. The two biggest sellers turned out to be featherbeds and the mattresses. Sandy arranged to have the sold mattress drop-shipped from the factory to the guest residence at no additional cost, but when Canadian guests made a mattress purchase, problems arose about shipping into Canada and that end of the business suffered.

"Other" visitors included contractors, of which some have already been mentioned. Early on, Sandy contracted with an interior decorator to redo the great room from a banquet hall to a homey parlor. Complete with sofas and game tables, where afternoon tea and scones could be served in front of the large fireplace. The room had to be easily converted back to a banquet hall to accommodate large weddings and other social gatherings. Part of the decorating scheme involved painting the long interior wall a muted yellow color which, when completed, turned out a blazing chartreuse. The decorator finally admitted she gave the wrong paint chip to the painter and paid to have the wall repainted, but not before some derogatory comments from guests and staff.

During the last year of our tenure at the Inn, we decided to proceed with remodeling the upstairs 1950's era apartment in the carriage house, which lay in disrepair from the remnants of an aborted attempt to make the area into guest rooms by the previous owner. Sandy's dad had drawn up blueprints for a two bedroom owner's quarters a few years earlier, and we finally had some spare cash and thought "why not". We also thought it might help sell the place, as the Inn had been on the market four years by that time. The first step was to rebuild the rickety open wooden staircase and small porch that led up to the apartment. We had heard good things about two brothers who were carpenters that lived close by and decided to ask them to design a staircase and give us a bid. We liked the design and creative little porch, and the price was reasonable.

They actually showed up on time, worked eight-plus hours a day, and came in on budget, a unique experience for us, in dealing with local contractors. They got excited about their little project and asked if they could bid on the apartment remodel itself, after we showed them the plans Sandy's dad had drawn up. We were pleased with the staircase and their work ethic and just told them to proceed with the project, per the budget we had established. As anticipated to some degree, they ran into some expected problems with an almost one hundred year old building, but also got carried away with their creative approach to building the master bathroom. The project dragged on and came in at twice the budget, but we were pleased with the results overall, and particularly with the unique cut stone counters and shower walls.

It was our intent initially to redo the main floor of the carriage house that was then being used for storage of ladders, landscape tools and equipment and whatever, into meeting rooms for group seminars/meetings. The basement area would then be cleaned up for storage needs. We stored Sandy's 1984 Mercedes on the main floor during the winter to keep it out of the snow and salt used on the roads. One spring when I uncovered the car to take it out of storage and back in service, I found the passenger seat sheepskin seat cover torn to shreds. I had left the windows open slightly for ventilation while under the cover and critters had gotten in and used the sheepskin to make nests. The car would not start and when I lifted the hood, I found most of the wires had been chewed and eaten, apparently by the same critters.

We used the Mennonite plumber that installed the gas logs in our Inn fireplaces to handle the plumbing aspects of the carriage house apartment project, which were considerable. I had interviewed three plumbing contractors for the gas logs before this man and all three told me that running gas lines was the same as running water lines, and even I knew that was not true. My bearded Mennonite plumber said he would not undertake such a job until the gas company came out and said it was o.k. to do so. He knew there was a difference and got the job. The gas log installation occurred during our first year of operation and he was our first experience with a contractor showing up on time and demonstrating a good work ethic. We soon learned that both the Mennonites and the Amish workers had this characteristic and we sought them out whenever possible.

The bearded one and his clean-shaven helper (only married men could have beards) showed up every morning and worked all day, stopping only to consume the lunch they each brought with them in their little black lunch pail. One day I was down in our apartment, adjacent to the game room, and heard the clink of pool balls. This was alarming as we did not have any guests that day. I yanked open the door to the game room to find our two Mennonite plumbers playing pool, a no-no in their faith. They were aghast and embarrassed no end. They had been working on the game room fireplace and just had to try out a pool table, said the bearded one. I volunteered a vow of secrecy and offered to let them finish their game, but they declined and returned to their task at hand. Another game room incident, different but somewhat related, involved an epidemic of fleas on the game room carpet. I watched TV down there one day while eating lunch and, upon returning upstairs, discovered my white athletic socks covered with black fleas. Investigation revealed a mass infestation of these little pests on the game room carpeted floor. How they had gotten there was a mystery until we found out that our yard man/gardener was coming to eat his lunch down in the game room. He was bringing them in from the yards on his clothing. We had to fog the room and had him eat lunch elsewhere.

We used this same team of plumbers on a guest room remodeling project that involved installing a porcelain old-fashioned claw-foot tub in a third floor attic-typed guest room. The tub weighed a ton, a fact we did not considered when purchasing it. How to get the tub up to the room became an issue, and my solution was to knock out a window, build a crane-type structure, and haul it up on the outside of the building. Easier said than done! While contemplating this solution, the bearded one offered to carry the tub on his back up the three flights in the back staircase. He was a big man, but not that big, and we were concerned both for his safety and for his dropping the tub down the stairwell. We decided to let him do it and he proceeded to place the tub on his back with the help of his partner. He was actually inside the tub and wore it like a turtle shell. With his partner steering him from the rear, he carried the tub up the three flights, into the guest room, and placed it gently on the tiled floor. An amazing feat!

But that was not all! While up in the huge attic to connect the remodeled room bathroom fixtures to the proper venting hardware, our bearded superman discovered that <u>all</u> nineteen bathrooms in the Inn were vented into a single large pipe that ran the length of the attic and vented into the chimney at the end of the building. That meant all sewer gasses were being vented into a hot chimney that, in turn, vented two large wood burning fireplaces. How the building survived that potential calamity for almost one hundred years is a miracle. Apparently, the architect did not want to penetrate the expensive Vermont tile roof and chose the chimney option instead. We were faced with the same dilemma and chose a third option, capping off the chimney exit and going out under the eaves.

Needless to say, we were enamored with our Mennonite plumbers. Unfortunately, being enamored worked both ways. The bearded one, who was considerably younger than Sandy and married with a mess of little ones, found Sandy to be irresistible and pursued her shamelessly. At first unobtrusively by bringing her flowers, but then blatantly by attempting to meet with her alone out at the carriage house project or showing up unannounced when I was away. Sandy was appalled and embarrassed, and made sure she was never alone with the poor man. He finally got the message and we ran out of plumbing projects at about the same time.

We contracted for some services and had some favorite providers that we enjoyed dealing with. Sandy identified a guest demand for in-room massage and after a trying out a few providers, settled on the wife of the swimming coach at the Academy. He was a long-term successful swim coach who trained a couple of kids who went on to become Olympic swimmers, one a gold medalist. His wife was a good masseuse, readily available because she lived in town, and had her own portable massage table. The only negative was that I had to carry the massage table from her car up to the guest rooms and back down again. We charged the massage to the room and paid the masseuse a set fee. Sandy got a free massage out of the arrangement now and then and I got a sore back from carrying the massage table up to the guest's room.

Our favorite provider was the husband/wife team that provided cooking classes once a quarter at the Inn. They ran a very successful Culinary Training School in Maryland, with him being French and her an American. He was a chef trained in France and she was the business manager who kept things going, both at the school and at the Inn cooking classes. We first met them the second winter at the Inn when a restaurant food supplier did a function at the Whitetail Ski Resort near the Inn, and took over most of our guestrooms for some clients of theirs. Among their guests were Patrice and Francois Dione, owners of the Academy De Cuisine in Bethesda, Maryland and friends of Julia Childs. Sandy struck up a friendship with them and attended a pastry cooking class at their facility later that year. While there, she convinced them to do the quarterly cooking classes at the Inn.

The Dione's would drive up to the Inn on Friday afternoon and do a "hands on" class Saturday morning for a class of ten to twelve guests, usually couples. The class would have lunch on the food they prepared that morning. That evening our chef would prepare a five-course prefix dinner for the class, Dione's, and us, which he hated because he felt he was being judged by Francois. The class had to reserve rooms for Friday and Saturday nights and the cooking class was part of a package. Many had taken demonstration classes at the Academy De Cuisine from Francois and relished the opportunity to be in the kitchen with him, as well as share a glass of wine with the Dione's on Friday and Saturday evening.

The first year or two, the Dione's would bring their youngest son, about twelve, with them to the Inn, and I would let him drive the Dixon riding lawnmower around the property, play with our German Shephard, or play pool. They said he looked forward to coming and did not seem to get bored.

Another package we provided was a "ski package" that combined a weekend stay with ski lift tickets for nearby Whitetail Ski Resort. It was not really a resort as it had limited overnight accommodations, but it was only a two-hour drive from Baltimore and D.C. Their shortage of overnight lodging was a windfall for the Inn and we were able to negotiate for discount tickets. We had to purchase a set number of non-refundable lift tickets in advance, however, so there was some risk on our part. Neither Sandy nor I ever got to ski there, but Megan learned to snowboard on their machine-made snow. The snow was mostly machine produced because there was not a lot of snowfall during the winter. The "ski resort" was developed by a Japanese corporation with little experience in such a venture. This became obvious when they built the ski runs on the southeast outside aspect of the cone-shaped volcano looking mountain. As such, it got full morning sun which quickly turned the snow made the night before to slush; which in turn became ice overnight. Early birds on the slopes had to deal with icy runs which turned to slush my noon. But then again, it was only two hours from D.C. and Baltimore.

Walt Filkowski

NOTABLE GUESTS

Whitetail brought us some of our most interesting guests. None could compare to the time Paul Newman and his wife, Joanne Woodward, stayed at the Inn, some years before we acquired it, however. The Japanese President of the holding company that built Whitetail came with his entourage for dinner one night, complete with a harpist that played a golden harp. We did not know if the harp was solid gold or not, but it was treated as such. They had dinner in the Rose Room, our private room for special dinners such as this, and dinner service became a real challenge. Some fifteen of his underlings had dinner with "the boss," but none of them could take a bite of anything until the boss did so first, apparently a Japanese business custom. If the boss got too chatty between bites, the rest of the party had to wait him out. This created a nightmare for the wait staff, who were trying to keep the soup warm or clear the table for the next course.

Another guest bought her teenage son and friend to ski over the weekend, taking advantage of our ski package, but paid her bill with a check written on a closed account. This was the first, and only, time that someone did this to us, and Sandy was not about to let her get away with it. When the woman refused to return all attempts at contacting her, Sandy turned the matter over to our intrepid Police Chief, Larry. Writing a check on a closed account is fraud, something Larry could sink his teeth into. He took the matter personally because a fraud was committed against someone in his town. He issued some kind of an intrastate warrant for her arrest and told Sandy it would only be a matter of time before she was apprehended. He also advised us to not take a credit card for payment, but to require cash for the bill and the returned check penalty. He also said he was leaving for a two-week vacation and nothing could be done until he returned, in the event the woman was arrested. Sure enough, she was pulled over in Maryland for a traffic stop later that week and taken to jail. Her estranged husband began calling to get her out of jail, but Larry had gone fishing and only he could authorize her release, after cash payment was received of course.

Larry finally returned some days later, and the mother of the boy that accompanied the mother/son on the ski weekend came to the Inn and paid the required cash amount.

One of our favorite guests was a seventy-two year old oriental man who was a chemist with the National Institute of Heath, In Washington, DC. We first met him as a guest of the vendor that put up some clients at the Inn while working a Whitetail Ski Resort event. He was a wiry little man who was a ski instructor on weekends and took our lobby stairs two at a time when going up to his room. He lived alone in town and would come to dinner every Thursday night for the prime rib special, following his initial visit as a guest of the vendor. He did not have a computer, television, telephone, or take the local weekly newspaper, and would satisfy these missing perks during his weekly visit. He would come early and read the paper in the great room, have dinner, and retire to the game room for some television time. He would ask to use the telephone or computer as the need arose. He always asked for the same waitress at dinner and would give her a few questions to research and answer at the next week's dinner. The waitress was a young part-time college student and he took an interest in her development. This went on for years, interrupted only by his attending the winter Olympics in Utah as a volunteer worker-bee. We invited him to attended our New Year's Eve function as our guest one year, thinking he would have dinner and leave because of his advancing age, but he stayed the entire evening and toasted the New Year with us.

Two of our guests turned out to be long-term resident businessman who needed a place to stay while their soon-to-be permanent residence was either being remodeled or purchased. The first was the new Head Master for the Mercersburg Academy located across the street from the Inn. His predecessor had held the position for many years and the Head Master's House on campus needed remodeling and updating badly. The new man stayed with us throughout the second summer of our tenure at the Inn while the remodeling project was being completed. He was a nice man, but somewhat stuffy and condescending. His head was always tilted slightly back as if he were sniffing the air. He wanted his breakfast each morning on our large porch outside the great room, in solitude. A slight inconvenience for the innkeepers, but possibly one reason why Megan was accepted as a student at the Academy, as only one of two local students they accepted each year.

The other long-termer was the new incoming President of the largest employer outside of Hagerstown, Maryland; JLG Industries. This company was located west over the mountain, in the small town of McConnellsburg, Pennsylvania, and manufactured man-lift apparatus such as mobile scissor-lifts and hydraulic telescoping cranes. They were a one billion dollar corporation by 2000 and the Mercersburg Inn was their guesthouse, special event, and restaurant of choice by then. His predecessor had been President for ten years and was the reason they used us. He lived in Hagerstown and had been to dinner at the Inn a couple of times since we had expanded the menu. The new President stayed with us while house-hunting and was an unusual replacement for the outgoing incumbent who was a quiet, reserved, and somewhat more cultured individual. While he appeared to have the professional qualifications, coming from a Fortune 500 company, the new man's social skills were a little suspect. He was divorced and had been living with his hairdresser girlfriend, who was straight out of the movie, "Grease." She came to visit him occasionally and was his date at a few of the JLG functions at the Inn. He was looking for a house somewhere between McConnellsburg and an Atlantic Ocean port where he could berth his seventy foot steel-hull yacht. That proved to be a lot of territory to cover, and I wondered if the time it took was more about each party looking at each other a little more closely.

The Inn needed external painting and brick repointing, so each summer I rented a JLG fifty foot hydraulic telescopic crane to reach the multistory areas on the Inn and the carriage house. The mobile crane was both driven and extended from the bucket itself and could reach anywhere, thus eliminate the need for ladders and extension ladders. The summer after our JLG quest had left, the rental place I usually rented from in Hagerstown did not have the unit and I reserved one from a new rental place In McConnellsburg that was affiliated with the JLG plant. When it did not show up on the appointed day, I called and was told that JLG did not make a 50 foot lift, but I could rent a 40 foot lift. I knew this not to be true, having rented a 50 foot lift in prior years, so I declined their offer and proceeded to rent a competing brand 50 foot lift from another vendor. Our former JLG guest liked Sandy's breakfast so much that he would stop in from time to time, on his way to work in the morning, to partake of whatever she was serving that day. JLG's lifts were painted orange and the competitor lifts were painted baby blue. As fate would have it, he came by for breakfast one morning and spied the baby blue lift in our parking lot. With visions of losing all future JLG business, I had to interrupt his breakfast and relate my story of why a baby blue lift was being used at the Mercersburg Inn. He accepted my explanation and actually called back that afternoon to say he had verified my story and had fired the person that claimed JLG did not make a 50 foot lift.

We continued to benefit from JLG business until we left the Inn, and partly as a show of good faith, purchased some JLG stock when they went public. That proved to be beneficial later on when JLG brought out their baby blue competitor and the stock rose somewhat. We would have benefited from another frequent guest had Megan decided to attend Wake Forest instead of Emory University in Atlanta. Upon graduation from the Academy in 2001 (another story), Megan wanted to become a veterinarian, but the best vet school in the country was at the University of California at Davis and impossible to get into. She decided to attend another UC campus in California and transfer up to the Davis campus after one year, as a possibility. She chose the UC campus at Santa Cruz, but after the year was up she became disenchanted with California in general, and decided that the Santa Cruz campus, and the whole UC system by means of the "guilt by association principle, was not a "learning environment". Apparently, the low cloud hanging perpetually over the coastal Santa Cruz campus was not fog, and both students and faculty smoked pot to the extent that, in some classes, windows had to be opened to let in fresh air. The fact 9-11 occurred during her freshman year away from home may have had something to do with her desire to return to the east coast and be closer to us.

Megan narrowed down her selection of east coast colleges to George Washington, Emory, and Wake Forest. George Washington did not take transfer students, so it became a decision between the other two, both of which were hard to get into. It turned out that one of our frequent guests was "Mr. Wake Forest", and he and his wife seemed to enjoy visiting with Sandy and myself. He was a below the elbow amputee on one side and would never let me carry his luggage up to their room. I never pressed him about his arm, even over a glass of wine or two, and he became comfortable enough with us to inquire about Megan's trials and tribulations concerning her college selection. She was leaning toward Wake Forest at this point which pleased our guest no end. We were never quite sure what our guest's connection with Wake Forest was; alumnus, benefactor, or administration, but he called one day and said Megan would be accepted if she applied.

I drove her down to North Carolina to visit the campus that summer, and while travelling along highway 72 we came upon a large overhead sign for the Winston-Salem turnoff. Megan said the signage reminded her of something and I said it was probably because of the cigarettes named for the town. I informed her that Wake Forest was founded by the cigarette company and her decision was made at that point. Our visit was brief and nothing about the campus was to her liking. She did not want to meet with anybody remotely connected with the school and the drive back home was a silent one. Megan had been anti-smoking since she could walk and talk and that was it! Emory became her choice and I had to pass that on to our guest, who we never saw again. Sandy has always claimed that Megan chose Emory because her sister, Lauri, lived within an hour driving distance, but I thought it was about tobacco.

Another interesting guest was a representative from a Federal Agency offering to pay for a new sewer system for the Borough. The Feds had a program designed to help small municipalities replace old ineffective sewer plants at little or no cost to the tax payer. I was on the town sewer commission at the time, so was familiar with our antiquated and broken sewer system that the Feds had mandated to replace. A member of the commission had invited the Feds to appear before the Borough Council and offer their proposal for replacing the existing sewer plant, at no expense to the Borough. It was a reed bed system with the residue being hauled off as fertilizer for the feed corn acreage surrounding the town, and a community park erected on the site of the old plant. The poor man was literally thrown out of the meeting with shouts of "there is no such thing as a free lunch". He came back to the Inn after the meeting mumbling to himself about the stupidity of these small town narrow minded bureaucrats. Six months later, with the Federal mandate timeline approaching, the borough council voted to replace the sewer system with a reed bed system at a cost of three million dollars, without the park of course. Sewer rates rose three times in less than a year, doubling at the third increase.

In the late 1990's, David Brooks, author of an article for the *Atlantic Monthly*, "One Nation, Slightly Divisible," in which he examined the county's cultural split following the 2000 national election, contrasted the red states that voted for bush and the blue ones for Gore. Brook's compared two counties: Maryland's Montgomery (Blue), where he lived, and Pennsylvania's Franklin (a Red country in a Blue state which housed the Mercersburg Inn). He made this comparison by means of a leisurely drive through Franklin County after crossing, what he termed "the Meatloaf Line", because he found fewer sun-dried –tomato dishes and a lot more meat loaf platters on restaurant menus. He went on to list a number of differences he found, such as, in Franklin County the women performed yard work on rider mowers and in his county they use illegal aliens, and a host of other perceived differences that denigrated Franklin County.

Another author took issue with what she termed "sweeping generalizations", and paid a visit to Franklin County to prove her point. She later wrote an article that debunked Brooks' generalizations, especially his allegation about not being able to spend more than twenty dollars on a meal. To quote an excerpt from her article;

> "The easiest way to spend over $20 on a meal in Franklin County is to visit the Mercersburg Inn, which boasts "turn-of-the century elegance." I had a $50 prix-fixe dinner, with an entrée of veal medallions, served with a lump-crab and artichoke tower, wild-pilaf and a sage—caper-cream sauce. Afterward, I asked the inn's proprietors, Walt and Sandy Filkowski, if they had seen Brooks' article.
>
> They laughed. After it was published, in the *Atlantic*, the nearby Mercersburg Academy boarding school invited Brooks as part of it's Speaker series. He spent the night at the Inn. "For breakfast I made a goat-cheese-and-sun-dried-tomato tart," Sandy said. "He said he just wanted scrambled eggs."

Brooks later had to admit to this author that "you can get a nice meal at the Mercersburg Inn". Both authors had stayed at the Inn and we receive some good publicity from their articles. The Academy, and the surrounding community, were geared up for Brooks talk and, apparently, gave him a hostile reception. We also received some much needed positive publicity in 2002 from a restaurant review service on the Web, *The Artful Diner*. Their two-page review of the Inn started off with a paragraph that seemed to support Brooks' first impression of Franklin County:

> *"When Walt Filkowski, proprietor of The Mercersburg Inn, is heard to remark that his is the only restaurant with white tablecloths within fifty miles, he may be exaggerating – but not a great deal. In point of fact, this particular area of the Keystone State is something of a gastronomic wasteland....which makes this lovely establishment such a remarkable find."*

The result of this free publicity may have been the reason for our first (and last) political guest at the Inn. One day we received a telephone inquiry from a front-man of a political organization, who wanted to know if we could provide an upscale $1000 per head fundraising reception complete with champagne, oysters, caviar, ice carvings, and the whole nine yards. We answered in the affirmative and set up a meeting with their event committee, who promptly downsized the event to cheap wine and a few hors d'oeuvres. The local candidate was running for a Congressional seat and needed to woo the Franklin County upper crust while separating them from their money. In exchange for this supposed financial windfall for the Inn and the exposure it would provide to the County movers-and-shakers, we would have to provide a guest room with three outside telephone lines for the candidate to conduct private meetings and make telephone calls.

On the day of the event, the candidate, and his entourage, arrived ahead of his schedule time and began a long list of demands. Worse than that was the arrival of his reception guests some two hours before the agreed upon time, when some of the hors d'oeuvres had not even been prepared or the wine opened. We were able to deal with all that, even with a prolonged delay of the candidate showing his face that extended the reception into the dinner hour. When he finally showed and made a brief speech from the lobby staircase, he apologized for the Inns inability to provide the upscale reception and dinner promised for their $1000 contribution, and promptly left for his next fund raising event over in the next county. We were shocked and subjected to numerous nasty comments from the attendees as they, in turn, departed in a huff.

In looking back, we should have suspected something like this after they downsized the menu and would not pay the required deposit until the morning of the event. We had to threaten them with cancelling the event before they wrote a check for the deposit. After the candidate's allegations in his speech, we worried that they might cancel payment on the check, which they did not. But they did drag out final payment on the balance due, until I threatened to go to the press with our version of what had occurred. It took us quite a while to overcome this adverse publicity, but we learned our lesson and never did a political event of any kind again.

Most Innkeepers universally agree that 90% of their guests are a delight and the other 10% can sometimes prove to be a challenge. During Parent Weekends at the Academy, we would often have to separate divorced parents, and their new significant others, to rooms at opposite ends of the Inn to prevent the possibility of embarrassment, or sometimes conflict. Even more difficult was seating arrangements at dinner, and breakfast was just impossible, especially if the kids were inviting over to join one set of parents. We had a frequent visitor couple from New York City who were somewhat unique, in that they would always look under the bed when first entering the room, and then go to the window and pull down the shades, before turning on any lights. When we asked about the shades, on their first visit, they explained that they lived on the top floor of a multi-story condo and had to be careful about snipers! When I told them the room overlooked a cemetery and probably did not have many visitors at night, let alone snipers, they insisted on having that room on every visit thereafter. They looked under the bed on every visit, but never explained why. We had to make sure there were no dust bunnies under the bed before each of their visits.

We had many interesting academy parents and got to know the parents of four- year students especially well. The mother of incoming freshman twin girls was referred to us by the Academy one day after she could not find a local accommodation that met her requirements. She was very British and her husband was very German, and they lived in a private compound in Hong Cong where the husband had an import-export business. They chose Mercersburg Academy to educate their girls and perfect their English because the Academy promised to have someone speak German to them every day, the language of choice at home. They had a condo in Washington, DC, a condo in New York City where their son attended Hunter College, and a house in Switzerland. The mother was used to upscale hotels and began making requests for personal items such as room service and laundry service. When she called down and asked me to take her coat out to a dry cleaner, we found it necessary to educate her on how B&B's and Country Inn's operated in the U.S.

Once we explained how things worked at the Inn, we expected her to move on, but much to our amazement she stayed on. I did accommodate her request for a television set in her room, with the provision she not tell the others guests and to keep the volume down. We were not looking forward to the husband arriving and making further requests that we could not honor, but he proved to be a really nice man who loved Sandy's breakfasts. The twins became the number one and two seeds on the tennis team as freshman, but had difficulty transitioning to living without servants. At some point, one of the girls was punished for not keep her room clean by having all of her possessions hauled out to the hallway. Mom had to intervene by cleaning the room herself. The other twin adapted to her new environment well, but the spoiled one was eventually pulled out of the school. Sandy became the sounding board for the mother, which she did for several of the parents on Academy issues, because they knew Megan was attending, or had attended.

Another Academy guest proved to be a "small world" story. He was an Academy alumnus and former Board Member who frequented the Inn when visiting his grandson at the school. On one visit he and I were talking and the subject of our living in California came up. He had attended Redlands University out there and we had played them in football long after he graduated. He commented that his daughter and her family still lived in the San Francisco Bay area and his son-in-law was a Chief x-ray technician at an East Bay hospital. One story led to another, and it turned out that his son-in-law was my Chief Tech when we took the labor strike at Oakland Hospital. He was one of the few department heads willing to cross the picket lines and even brought his wife in to help out. When his grandson graduated from the Academy, he brought his daughter and her husband, my Chief Tech, out from California to stay at the Inn. The grandfather was also a professional photographer and gave us a beautiful book of Pennsylvania pictures he had taken and published. In fact, he gave us two of the books after the original was taken from the Inn, and he replaced it when he found out.

The Board of Trustees for the Academy met quarterly and we were the accommodation of choice for them, being right across the street from the school. They served a four-year-term, so we got to know them pretty well, particularly their preference for breakfast. Sandy would make whatever they wanted, from egg white omelet s to Palisade Poached Pears. They rarely brought their wives along and treated the visit as just another business trip. They would come in the night before their Board Meeting, have dinner that night on campus, breakfast at the Inn, and leave right after the meeting. They were all Academy Alumni and successful businesspeople that had made generous monetary contributions in the past. The female Olympic Gold Medalist swimmer was appointed to the Board the year before we left the Inn.

Another interesting guest was a country club golf professional who showed up at least once a month with a different lady. On the second visit, he pulled me aside and requested that none of the Inn staff mention that he had ever been a quest before. The ladies were always tens on a 0-10 scaled and often paid the bill when they departed. After six or seven visits, he never appeared again and we assumed an irate husband may have intervened.

Before 9-11, many of our regular guests were businesspeople and most of these were dealing with JLG. The females preferred the Inn over motels because of security issues and the men seemed to like the casual atmosphere of wandering around the Inn with drinks in front of the big fireplace or playing pool or darts in the game room. They could have dinner with us or walk downtown to dine or drink without having to drive. That created a problem for me sometimes because they would expect me to stay up to drink and converse until the wee hours. I would then have to get up early the next morning to help with breakfast and do checkouts. Of course, both male and female liked the reduced room rates we offered to mid-week business-related guests. A lot of the businessmen were with a paint company, based in Atlanta, Georgia, that had the paint contract for JLG. Paint was a major contract and JLG had strict guidelines that had to be met, and there always seemed to be paint-related issues that required their presence.

When the Twin Towers came down, business travel on the East Coast came to a halt, and we never saw many other businesspeople again. No one wanted to fly anywhere for a long time after 9-11.

Occasionally, we would get a businessperson in town to service the Academy and one, in particular, ended up helping us out. He was a financial advisor who helped the Academy out with their $250 million dollar endowment fund. He loved the Inn and brought his wife back a few times. Sandy worked out a bartering arrangement, whereby, he provided us with retirement financial planning in exchange for free stays at the Inn. Bartering was something Innkeepers did frequently, particularly in the northeast, but one had to be wary of IRS implications. At the time we were doing our retirement financial projections, we were earning ten percent interest on our money market funds and this man wanted to use that percentage going forward into the future. Fortunately, conservative Sandy talked him down to six percent, and even that number proved not conservative enough when 2007 hit.

Our last guest worth mentioning was actually a group of guests. A Maryland attorney was going to celebrate his 50th birthday by jogging 50 miles along the path along the Chesapeake and Ohio (C and O) Canal, along with a group of his attorney friends. The C and O was built in the 1850's and ran for 184.5 miles from Washington, DC, to Cumberland, Maryland, parallel to the Potomac River. His stretch of jogging was going to be from somewhere around Harpers Ferry, Maryland, to Williamsport, Maryland; some 45 minutes from the Inn.
They reserved several rooms for the night and took over the sun porch for dinner.

Sometimes the best of plans do not work out. He ended up jogging only ten of the fifty miles with only one of his attorney friends, while the rest electing to show up early at the Inn to drink, in lieu of jogging. He and his jogging friend showed up later and caught up to his friends drinking-wise in a hurry. Dinner included a dress up affair, of World War II era uniforms for the men and formal attire for the females in attendance, and a lot of wine. After a boisterous dinner they retired to the large porch adjacent to the great room for cigars and more drinks. When the bar closed at 2: am, and after several warning to keep to noise down, they remained on the porch with their own private bottles and the noise level increased. My final warning included a threat to call in the police and the attorneys joked about our 1 ½ man police force. So, I called Larry and explained the situation about the complaining neighbors and Inn guests, and he showed up ten minutes later.

Larry took one look at the porch full of loud-mouthed inebriated male and female attorneys and gave them a quick option. Go to bed with no more disturbances inside or outside the Inn, or, be arrested on the spot for drunk and disorderly and be taken up to the next large town (Chambersburg) with the assistance of the State Police, to await arrival of the circuit judge two or three days from then. Transfer was necessary because his jail (a closet with a curtain) was too small for all of them. The noise stopped immediately, as the attorneys began to drift off the porch in ones and twos, except for the birthday boy holdout who tried to impress me by hurling one or two final insults at Larry, before departing for his room. I think that, if any of them could have driven, they would have taken off for home....after Larry had left that is. Breakfast the next morning was sparsely attended by the attorney contingent, and check-out was a painful process for all concerned. Later that day while cleaning up the porch of half-smoked and barely smoked cigars that the female attorneys had tried to smoke in an effort to keep up with their male counterparts, Sandy came to me in tears because someone (guess who) had cut up the bridle and saddle of the large wooden rocking horse her dad had made for Megan that we had displayed in the game room. One of the attorneys used these items to make his/her uniform for dinner.

Growing Old in America

I guess one of our favorite guests was one who never came at all, in spite of numerous invitations and even a gift certificate. That would be Larry the Police Chief, of course. Larry lived In Mercersburg his whole life and was considered a local. He was tall and thin and Sandy called him String Bean. We probably got off on the right foot with him, when I gave the boy he was concerned about a job cutting the lawns when I first arrived. After he helped us with the bad check incident, Sandy presented him with a gift certificate and planted a big kiss on his cheek at the three-way intersection downtown while he was directing school bus traffic. I am sure he was embarrassed to death to have this done in public view. He later helped us with the attorney incident and also with a troubled employee who turned out to be an alcoholic. One Christmas this front desk employee asked if she could spend Christmas Eve in the Inn with her young daughter since we closed the Inn to visit our daughter in Georgia. The Inn was decked out for Christmas with three decorated trees and other decorations and she thought her daughter would be thrilled. We agreed, but upon returning found out she opened the Inn to her friends for a party. They slept in and used the guest room beds for other purposes and drank up some beer and wine. A week later I responded to a dinner guest complaint that the martini I had made him did not have any vodka in it. Our then former employee had drunk a fifth of vodka and replaced it with water. Larry tracked her down and we agreed not to press charges because of her condition and situation.

Larry was an Andy Griffin fan and built a replica of the 1960ish Ford Galaxy 500 used on the Andy Griffin Show in the 1960's. He was very proud of that car and drove it in the Halloween parade every year. He also drove it down to Mount Airy, North Carolina, the home town of Andy Griffin and the place the fictional town of Mayberry was based, every summer. He also built a replica of the pick-up truck used in the television show Sanford and Son of 1960's vintage also. Someone else drove this replica in the parade. I never had the heart to tell Larry that the Ford Galaxy used in the show changed every year with an updated model. It was always a four-door Galaxy provided by a local dealer, but not the same car throughout the five year running of the show.

Larry never did use his gift certificate or take anything from us for all the help he provided the Inn. He was appreciated locally for his honesty and helpfulness, as evidenced when a move to combine all the local borough police departments into a single county agency was met with "but what will happen to Larry?" If nothing else, Larry will always be remembered for his recollection and telling of the infamous "funeral home burglary", to be told later.

COMMUNITY INVOLVEMENT

We knew from the start that one, or both, of us would have to get involved in the local community as soon as possible, especially with the Academy. We did some of this in the purchase of the Inn through interaction with the City Manager, Borough Council and Mayor; and Academy through Jim Smith, friend of the previous owner who ran the music department at the Academy and owner of the building the state leased for its liquor store. Being first on the scene BS (before Sandy) I initiated involvement by purchasing the Suburban locally and continuing the relationship with the local food market for small purchases. I joined the local Chamber of Commerce and even utilized two of the local men's barber shops, in hopes of starting some dialogue with the locals. The first shop was manned by an old man who used the squeeze clippers for five or six passes over my head that took three or four minutes and charged me $10. The second shop used electric clippers that took less time and cost more. He almost shaved my head completely a day or two before I went to get my new Pennsylvania driver's license, and be recorded on film for the next seven years. In both instances, I sat and waited in silence as no one present spoke a word. I had also become friendly with the Police Chief by hiring the kid he recommended to cut our lawns.

The driver's license experience is worth mentioning. The office itself was in an isolated part of the county in a small building with a big parking lot. The large parking lot was needed because the line to the single clerk extended out of the building and wrapped around the parking lot. This local branch of the DVM used handicapped workers to staff the license renewal window and, on this day, it was a young lady with Downs Syndrome. She was proficient enough at her job except for one problem. You could have your picture taken as many times as you wanted until you had one you liked. This slowed down the process considerably, particularly with female drivers. As much as I disliked my picture with the almost shaved head, there was not anything to be gained by having my picture taken again.

After Sandy, Megan, and the pets arrived, community interaction increased significantly. Megan was registered for middle school, the pets went to the local vet, and the three two-legged residents hooked up with the local General Practitioner. Later, we found out that our local GP had miss-diagnosed the former Inn owner's cancer and that ended our relationship. I began playing poker with some of the Academy faculty, including Jim Smith, which led to my being asked to serve on the Borough Sewer Commission. I soon learned that Mr. Smith, who also sat on the Sewer Commission, had orchestrated my selection as a member to serve as an ally. He served on the Sewer Commission to make sure the Academy, the largest user of the sewer system, was not adversely impacted by any future decisions involving rate increases or assessments. This, in itself, was a little strange because sewer rates were a factor of water usage, and the Academy had a series of wells on its 300 acres that kept public water use to a minimum. Their kitchen and human waste amounts were considerable, and the Inn, when busy, was probably second in this regard. While I did not publicly back his stand on some issues before the commission, I did not oppose him either. This paid off when I got his support, along with the City Managers, to sink a well, for irrigation-purposes-only, on Inn property, after wells within city limits were banned. Of course, when the well-digger commenced drilling, a crowd of locals showed up to protest this violation of the ordinance prohibiting such a thing, and I had to explain our exemption.

Sandy and I, and sometimes Megan, would try to patronize the local town and surrounding area restaurants, which ranged from O.K. to awful. The town breakfast place was among the O.K. establishments because it was the only place around that served coconut crème pie. We got friendly with the waitress and she would keep us posted on how we stood with the locals. She had told us that it took about thirty years of residence before one would be considered a "local". After a year or two, the waitress told us that the town had essentially accepted us after figuring us out. We were obviously in the witness protection program because we had "all that money" to buy the Inn, and who else would leave California to come to Mercersburg! I confided to the waitress that I was not Jimmy Hoffa, should that situation ever come up. I did not tell her that the price we paid for the Inn was only a couple of hundred thousand dollars more than we sold our house for in California.

We patronize two other eating establishments in town. One was owned and operated by a single lady and located on the town square. Her main attraction was chicken wings. The Academy students frequented it a lot as an alternative to their dining hall and also because the price was right, at 25 cents a wing. They also frequented the local pizza parlor, which was the old train station converted into a long narrow restaurant. The owners of the pizza joint allowed the students to smoke on site and also provided a warning system, in the event a faculty member wandered by. Smoking was a dismissal event, on or off campus.

The other restaurant was located half-way down the block and also had a few guest rooms that were mostly rented out during parent' weekend. The owners were a Romanian man and his American wife who had been the "other party" allegedly interested in buying the Inn before we showed up. His story was that he was living in Romania during the revolution and coup in December of 1989. He was a friend of the executed communist leader and fled to the United States, where he was currently hiding in Mercersburg. I immediately thought he was Jimmy Hoffa because he had a lot of money to buy the restaurant in town. Their menu was a little more varied that the chicken wing place and probably came in second to our Inn.

There were two other places in town that were bars that served food and it had to do with obtaining a state liquor license. Only so many liquor licenses were allowed in a defined area, but exceptions were made if a certain percentage of your total revenue was food related. Our Inn had one of these licenses' and we had to report this breakdown of food to alcohol annually. All of us had full bars
And, I assumed that is why the State, in its wisdom, placed a liquor

store in Mercersburg. We all purchased some, but not all, of our wine and liquor from the local store, keeping in mind that the Maryland and West Virginia state lines were only twenty minutes away and Virginia only 45 minutes away.

Another restaurant experience led to some negative publicity and maximum embarrassment. Whenever there were not any room reservations and not a dinner night, Sandy and I would take this opportunity to get away from the Inn and go out to dinner. On such a night we drove around to some local rural restaurants, only to find that none took credit cards and we did not have enough cash for dinner. At the third or fourth place, Sandy went in to ask about credit cards and return with a negative response. I backed out of the parking space in a huff and backed into a light pole. I jammed the transmission into drive, hit the gas and the suburban shot ahead and drove through the restaurant front door. The engine was racing and the back wheels spinning despite my foot on the brake. I had to turn off the key to shut down the engine, and assumed the gas pedal had stuck to the floorboard.

The police and fire department responded and no was hurt, but there was significant damage to the building and the restaurant eventually had to close down. Needless to say, we made the front page of the local papers the next day with an inference that I had rammed the restaurant after being denied use of a credit card for dinner.

The local newspapers often found it difficult to come up with front page material and some of what they published was classic. Deer hunting was very popular all over Pennsylvania, and most all the business community gave the opening of Deer Season off as vacation for their workers, because they would not show up anyway. Even the public schools gave the first two days of deer season off, for the kids, and the faculty, to go hunting. You could count on the local papers to run front page stories on some aspect of deer hunting during this period, and two of my favorite stories came from the front pages. The first involved a female deer hunter who sat up in her tree deer blind, with a case of beer, waiting for an unsuspecting deer to wander by. When a deer finally wandered by, she stood up and fired off a round from her big bore rifle, and the recoil knocked her out of the tree blind. The fall resulted in a broken hip, but she managed to crawl some twenty yards and tag the deer before passing out. There was not any mention of her blood alcohol content.

The other favorite story came after Thanksgiving and involved a man suing his wife for throwing the Thanksgiving turkey out the window during an argument at the dinner table. He alleged personal trauma from that event and the future loss of turkey sandwiches and turkey soup, because the family dogs had devoured the cooked bird. A follow-up story indicated a judge had thrown the suit out of court for being frivolous. And a runner-up for best front page story was a detailed account of a minor tornado that came through Hagerstown, Maryland, and tore off roofs of buildings and uprooted large trees. The paper went great lengths to say it was only a wind shear, because nobody had been killed or injured. I suspected the local Chamber of Commerce had edited that story.

Other community involvement included participation in the annual Town fair, Townfest, and attendance at the annual Borough Fair and County Fair. We had a booth at Townfest and sold items from our gift shop. In Pennsylvania, every small municipality has a fair, followed by a County fair, and ending up the summer with the State Fair. Our Borough Fair had the rides and games and food booths that attracted folks from the outlying farms and nearby hills of West Virginia. These were people you only saw once a year, at Fair-Time, and it was just as well. Families would come down from the hills with a mess of barefoot kids, who were often afflicted with Down's Syndrome from inbreeding, and steal anything that was not nailed down. When I inquired from a town local how they survived up in the hills, he told me they lived mostly off of deer meat. When I commented that would be hard to do on just one or two deer- kill medallions a year, he laughed and said no law enforcement person in their right mind would go up in those hills and check on medallions.

We also patronized a swimming lake in the summer, up in the mountains toward McConnellsburg that had a nice beach. The first time we were up there, we were surprised when they blew a whistle and ordered everyone out of the water. They did this every hour-on-the-hour to make sure no one had drowned. Megan went up to the ski resort several times to snow board and meet boys, and I played the links course in the summer there once or twice. There was not much opportunity for play or entertainment during the early years at the Inn.

INN PETS

We had a "No Pet" policy at the Inn, as did most of the hospitality industry at the time, but we did so partly because we had our own pets on the premises. Megan had her cat, Mittens, and we had our family German Shepherd, Sheba. The two pets were quite friendly and often slept together in a pile. Mittens was an indoor/outdoor cat and, after a brief orientation period, had the run of our cellar apartment and the five-acre property. Occasionally, someone would leave a door open and he would get up into the Inn, necessitating a search that usually found him lying on one of the guest room beds. A bad habit that he developed involved hunting baby rabbits and bringing them screaming back down to our basement apartment. During our first fall season at the Inn, Sandy uncovered a nest of baby rabbits along the winding path leading from the parking lot to the Inn, while planting flowers. She told Megan about them and cautioned her about Mittens proclivity for such critters. Somehow Mittens got out and the next morning came home with a screaming baby rabbit. Sandy and Megan were horrified and rushed out to find only two of the litter remaining alive. Megan promptly adopted the pair and raised them until they were able to fend for themselves.

We assumed the mother rabbit had fallen prey to the resident great horned owl that lived on our five-acre property. He could be seen perched on one of the second floor balcony railings early in the morning, after dining on the small animals that shared the estate the previous evening. Later that year, Mittens suddenly developed an aversion for outdoor activity. Once he could not wait to be let out, but overnight he would scratch and howl if picked him up to take out to the stairs leading up to the driveway. There was an old hawk that hung out in the trees by the carriage house, but more likely the horned owl had made a pass at Mittens, and the hunter had become the hunted. It took months before Mittens would venture outside again. Instead, he sought solace by latching on to whoever was in the apartment at the time, usually Megan. But when Megan went off to college, I became his buddy. When I retired to my recliner in the basement to eat lunch and watch Northern Exposure on T.V., Mittens would curl up on my lap and we would both take a nap. The summer I went to California to be with Megan and Sandy flew out to join us, Mittens died. The Vet thought he became depressed from loneliness and just died.

Meanwhile, the Great Horned Owl decimated everything smaller than itself on the five acres, and moved across the street to the Academy. When Megan returned from California after her freshman year, Mittens was replaced with Sasha, the devil cat. This black cat proved to have split personalities over the years, and remained an indoor cat while at the Inn. One of her peculiar activities involved waiting in hiding on a pile of boxes, stacked behind the apartment entrance door off the back staircase, when she heard me coming down the back stairs. When I came through the door, she would wait and jump onto my upper back and neck as I passed through. It scared the hell out of me the first few times, but eventually became a game, until Megan left for college in Georgia and took Sasha with her.

Being located on the highest point in town, we were subjected to the violent thunder and rain storms that plagued the area during the summer. After one violent wind storm, Megan found two baby crows on the ground under the row of tall pine trees on our property. The strong wind had tossed them out of their nest and they were calling out to their parents, who were responding in kind, but unable to do anything for them. Megan scooped them up and cared for them until they were strong enough to rejoin their parents, who remained nearby the whole time.

About a year before we left the Inn, a large pure white cat with blue eyes appeared on the deck outside the Inn kitchen door. It had thick fur like a bear instead of hair and refused to leave when confronted by the German Shephard. We told the kitchen staff, especially the chef, not to feed the cat or it would not leave. Our instructions fell on deaf ears and the cat enjoyed fine dining whenever Sandy and I were out of sight. We finally gave up and decided to keep it, and Sandy tried calling it by several names before we gave it a label. The cat responded to Charlie and he became the Inn cat thereafter. Charlie enjoyed riding in a car and especially enjoyed lying on the front dashboard underneath the windshield. Whenever I drove down to the bank to make a deposit at the drive through window, the teller would have a treat for Charlie. A problem soon developed, however, when Charlie would somehow get into the guest cars just before they were leaving the Inn. More than one guest had to return, open a car door, and eject Charlie out onto the driveway.

Sheba, our German Shephard, became the official "Inn Dog" and was a part of the Mercersburg Inn experience as much as Sandy or I. She greeted guests on the winding path from the parking lot to the Inn and checked out vendors and service people that came on official business. Reminiscent of her days guarding the circle drive of our Santa Rosa House, I took a telephone call one day from a guest parked out in our parking lot asking me to come get the dog lying out by the path leading to the Inn. He was an African American gentleman and apparently sensed Sheba's dislike for people of color. We had her from six weeks old and never could understand where she got this trait. Sheba always accompanied me outside when I did yard work, and after the first time I rolled the riding lawn mower over on myself trying to cut the terraced lawn, she would come and sit at the top of the rock driveway that circled the front of the Inn to be available should I do it again (which I did at least two more times). Sheba was not any help when I drove off the curb while cutting the narrow strip between the sidewalk and the road. I somehow fell off the seat and got wedged in on the floorboard as we traveled onto highway 16 among the truck traffic. It was a sad day when we had to have her put down by the vet at age fifteen and no longer able to function. We had to call all our kids to get permission to do so, and the vet, his tech, and myself were all crying when the injection was made.

And Megan had her horse, old Gus. The couple she helped care for, and show, their miniature horses found her a gentle older horse that was blind in one eye. The couple had their own regular horses that they liked to ride and I think they wanted Megan to be able to ride with them, especially the wife. They did not have any kids of their own and had sort of adopted Megan. They even provided a saddle, blanket, and bridle for the horse. They could ride from the stables down some back alleys onto the Inn property to visit us. The cellar of our carriage house was set up for horses originally, and with a little fixing up could have housed old Gus, had Megan's interest in horses continued. But, alas, as mentioned before, once she started school at the Academy, her interest changed to the two-legged stallions.

The last critter worth mentioning was not a pet, but a fowl visitor. One morning Sandy called me outside, where she had been working in her herb garden, to witness the arrival of a huge male turkey in full plume walking up our driveway. He strolled up the driveway around to the carriage house and disappeared down around the back. It was the largest turkey either of us had ever seen, his head being as tall as mine, and we never saw him again.

Growing Old in America

DESIGNATED INN STORY-TELLER

I became the official Inn local historical story-teller largely because of my duties at the front desk, breakfast server, bartender, restaurant Maître D', and my all-around charm and personality. Guests were starved for local history because the whole town was a designated historic district and was located in the hotbed of civil war history. Throw in the Academy with its religious beginnings and Jimmy Stewart attendance, the town being the birthplace of a U.S. President, and you have a wealth of information available to be told and retold; sometimes accurately, but other times slightly embellished. I fell privy to much of this information by word-of-mouth from the locals, as well as from books such as **OLD MERCERSBURG**, a book first assembled and published in 1912 by The Woman's Club of Mercersburg and reprinted several times over the years.

Guest's also wanted to know about Sandy and my background, and how we got into innkeeping. They all professed to always having wanted to own and operate a Bed and Breakfast, and they all suffered from what Sandy and I referred to as the "Bob Newhart Syndrome". Years before, Bob Newhart was in a television sit-com in which he owned and operated a small B&B and interacted with guests at his front desk and lobby area. Never once did you see him clean a toilet, make a bed, or cook breakfast. This was how most people saw owning a Bed and Breakfast was; someone else doing all the nasty stuff while you sat around hobnobbing with the guests.

Sandy and the wait staff would just roll their eyes and shake their heads whenever I launched into one of my stories, when it came out slightly different than the last time they heard me tell it. In defense of this, however, in most instances a story only was forthcoming in answer to a question asked of me by the guest. Most of my stories involved civil war activity, especially about Jeb Stuart's visit to Mercersburg during the Gettysburg battle. A popular tale shared by the guests themselves, and verified by our own experience, was traveling along Highway 30 alongside the Gettysburg battlefields and getting this weird chilling feeling. But my all-time story always enjoyed, and seemingly never believed, by the guests was the funeral home safe theft story. This story was told to me by Larry, our Police Chief, and verified several times at our poker games over at the Academy. I was invited early-on to play poker with several of the Academy male faculty because they smelled new money. They bled me the first few months by playing a game new to me, three-card Alabama, but I caught on eventually and held my own thereafter.

As the story unfolded, a young man moved into Mercersburg, from one of the thousand nearby municipalities, to work one of the local farms during their feed corn harvest. He rented a room looking out over one of the town's narrow back streets on which sat the town funeral home. The funeral home office was located directly across the street from this man's rented room and he had a clear view of the office; especially a view of the large stand-a-lone safe on rollers that sat in the corner. What caught his attention was the door to the safe always being open and large amounts of paper money piled loosely into and lying partly out of the safe. The word around town was that the elderly funeral home owner (in his 80's) left the safe open because he had lost the combination. Every day the farm worker would look into that window and occasionally see the old man throw a wad of bills into the safe, or at least toward the open door.

Such an opportunity was apparently too good to pass up, so he enlisted the help of three of his friends from home to steal the money. One early morning at about 2 a.m., the four thieves entered the office and one of them scooped up the loose money on the floor into the safe and shut the door…which locked! There was some conjecture on whether or not this was by design, but now the only way to get the money was to take the safe. They backed up an older muscle car, with the huge trunk, to the back door and rolled the big safe out the door, down the steps and into the trunk; covering it with a blanket and tying the half-open trunk to the bumper. Chief Larry claimed taking the safe was the original plan, but that is hard to believe with the door already open and the money there for the taking. One problem that surfaced immediately was that the rear of the car rode only a few inches off the ground with the weight of the safe and four people in the car.

Supposedly, they rode around town for a while trying to figure out what to do with the safe (which contradicts having had a plan to steal it originally), and were stopped by the night shift policeman/assistant Chief who thought they looked suspicious driving around at that hour. Really! He questioned the driver, but did not have a reason to detain them and sent them on their way. He did, however, take down the driver's name and address, which turned out to be accurate. The thieves drove the safe into nearby West Virginia while traveling, in mostly daylight, with a now partially covered safe sticking out of the trunk. They drove to a friend's trailer home because he had a high powered drill that could penetrate the safe (sounds like a plan to me). Now they would have to split the proceeds five ways instead of four ways. While drilling the safe, they sent one of the gang back to Pennsylvania with the muscle car to hide it and return with a different vehicle for their ultimate escape.

The safe was drilled open minus the fifth man present, and to their dismay, the amount of cash was less than expected. Instead, they found bearer bonds (as good as cash money) and stock certificates (which could have been sold) worth an estimated one million dollars. These items were promptly burned as being useless. Even these morons could figure out that having to split less cash more ways was not an attractive option, so they split the money four ways and took off in the trailer man' car for Disney World....Yes, Disney World! When the fifth man returned and found they had left with his share, he got mad and decided to rat them out. It took Chief Larry a while to figure things out because his night officer was unaware a burglary had occurred until he arrived for work early the next evening and shared his suspicious stop with the Chief. It then became a matter of waiting for the other four to return from Disney World, after spending all the stolen money on booze and

Walt Filkowski

Mickey Mouse.

There were several holes in this story, that some of our guests delighted in pointing out to the story-teller, that being me. The most glaring was that, if he observed the money in an open safe, why did the original man in the apartment not just go in at night and steal the money? Another questioned why he needed three additional men to steal the money from an open safe. Chief Larry alleged that a rumor had circulated that the safe contained gold bars, thus the need to take the safe???? In any event, it would have made a great movie, with Don Knotts and Tim Conway in leading roles.

Another story involved the Academy and involved model trains. Many years ago, a young Mercersburg man worked at the Academy and lived with his widowed mother in town. He loved model trains and. unbeknownst to his mother, started a train layout in the attic of their house. He never learned to drive when the horseless carriage made its appearance and could not afford a horse before that time. He walked, and later rode a bicycle, into Maryland, Virginia, West Virginia, and most of Pennsylvania to buy an engine, or car, or piece of track for his layout.

He worked at the Academy for 30 years and when he died, left his formidable model train collection to the Academy. The Academy's problem was finding a suitable location on campus for the collection and layout, and the problem became greater when alumni began leaving their collections to the school when word got out. An older building was finally remodeled and some local alumni model train enthusiasts were enlisted to run the whole show. It is truly a wonderful collection of Lionel trains, in particular.

A town story involved the original town fountain that sat in the middle of the town square and formed a kind of a modern day "around-about" traffic diversion. The now highway 16 travels straight through town and connects Green Castle on highway 81 to the east with McConnellsburg to the west. Over the years, trucks became more prevalent everywhere and also larger in size, so that movement around the fountain became more difficult and certainly slowed down traffic. A town ordinance was even passed prohibiting trucks from "jake breaking" to slow themselves down when going down the hill in front of the Inn. "Jake breaking" was dropping the transmission manually in progressively lower gears to slow down the truck, without using the brakes, and was quite noisy.

Apparently, the trucking fraternity became irritated with Mercersburg for its anti-trucking attitude and one morning the town awoke without a fountain in its square. What happened remained a mystery for many years, until the fountain appeared one day in the back yard of a residence bordering the Academy, where it can be seen today. This was a good-sized fountain and it had to take some planning and resources to have it disappear and reappear without somebody local knowing something about it, but nobody talked about it the eight years we lived there.

I could fill a book with Mercersburg stories alone, but these were a few of the more notable ones. The fact that the Borough kept a MacDonald's out of the town limits for over twenty years until the Mayor retired and sold them the land he owned, at a then much inflated price, to build on; or when the owners of the nearby ski resort and golf course put the resort up for sale and the Borough was going to float a bond issue to purchase and operate it, made excellent stories to tell the guests.

Walt Filkowski

BURNED OUT OR JUST BORED

About year two of being innkeepers, when most of the improvements and upgrades were completed, we began to think about an exit strategy and pursuing other interests. When our favorite antique warehouse went up for sale, we thought about buying it and running both entities. The owner wanted too high a price, however, and we could not make it pencil out. I missed the wheeling and dealing aspect of my last job at Summit so, when the two elderly gay women that owned and operated the Bed and Breakfast Industry professional organization, PAII, was rumored to be wanting out, I contacted them about taking over. The Professional Association of Innkeepers International was comprised of most, if not all of the B&B's and Inns in the United States, Canada, Mexico, and a few in other countries. It was beginning to lose membership during the first few years of our participation due, in part, to the age of the people running it and the lack of change. It became the same old thing year after year and dependent on volunteers to staff the annual meeting and year-long programs.

It was about the same time we became members of Select Registry/Distinguished Inns of North America that the rumors about PAII began to surface. When I contacted the PAII owners, they referred me to Select Registry because they too had expressed an interest in taking over. Select Registry actually contacted us first and we began a dialogue about how best to acquire the PAII operation. It boiled down to SR having the money, but not the resources to operate it and Sandy and I had the operational skills, but not the money. At one point SR was going to purchase The Mercersburg Inn from us and we would, in turn, purchase PAII with the proceeds and run it. The newly appointed Select Registry CEO and a Board Member and I agreed to meet in Cleveland to put together a proposal, but they arrived with other parties and an attorney, and I walked in on a meeting I felt was already in progress. We had a nice dinner and they picked my brain some more which, it turned out they had been doing all along. A few months later SR announced their acquisition of PAII without ever telling us beforehand.

Had SR not become our number one guest referral source through their guidebook, we would have dropped out.

Meanwhile, Sandy began tutoring trigonometry over at the Academy and was asked to sit on a committee advising the Borough on the feasibility of purchasing the nearby resort golf course and possibly the ski operation. A consultant had convinced the Borough Council to float a Municipal Bond Issue with a D/F rating, which amounted to "Junk Bonds." The Academy CFO and Sandy were the "lone voices in the night" that advised the Council against the Bond Issue and the purchase. A small Borough of 1500 people buying and operating a ski/golf resort was unimaginable. Fortunately, the consultant ran a trial balloon to see how many bonds would be sold, and the result was almost none. Case closed with no purchase! Chief Larry was disappointed because he had already planned on expanding his police department by two men.

During this same time period, I received a telephone call from my last boss at Summit, Irwin, and he offered me a job. It would have been a "black hat" opportunity to turn around another East Bay hospital. Shortly after I left Summit, our nemesis and largest competitor, based in Berkeley, had been purchased by the Sutter Group. Before I left, I had initiated discussions with the Berkeley hospital about a possible merger, but Irwin had turned his nose up at the idea, as he had done about us taking over the County Hospital. He always wanted to go it alone and be the big fish in a little pond. But Sutter was not content with just taking over Berkeley and made a move on Oakland and Summit Medical Center. They apparently bypassed Irwin and went straight to the Board. Irwin saw the handwriting on the wall and elected to leave and take on another "turn around project". His only problem was he did not have a Filkowski to do his dirty work. I talked it over with Sandy and we decided to stay put at the Inn.

A guest inquired about the colored glass ceiling lights in the foyer and dining room and, upon further inspection, declared them to be

Tiffany light fixtures of possible significant value. We had been told they were Tiffany, but did not think of them as priceless. There were also three large millstones down by the front edge of the property that someone had placed there as stepping stones up to the sidewalk. One day while I was managing to stay on the riding mower while cutting the grass, a man came by and offered to buy the millstones if we ever decided to leave the Inn. He said they probably came from some of the 1700's flour mills that dotted the local area and were historical pieces. I thanked him for the information and said I would contact him, if and when. This got us to thinking about possibly selling off some of the historical and valuable items in the Inn to raise capital for our next venture. Neither item turned out to have enough value to be worth pursuing, however.

We also considered moving out of the basement about this time and getting off the property entirely. The old house adjacent to our parking lot, that used to sit on the Inn site, was in disrepair and occupied, and not far enough away. Remodeling the carriage house was a huge undertaking and would have been both expensive and time-consuming. There was a nice looking house on 100 acres on the way up to the ski resort that we always admired, so we contacted the local realtor and found out it was for sale. The realtor was very familiar with the house, as it had been on the market forever. It was a good news-bad news scenario, with the good news being the price and the fact the 100 acres could be leased for farming, at a price that would almost cover the mortgage. The bad news was that the farm was previously owned by two elderly brothers who disliked each other quite a lot. So much so that they divided the house equally and lived apart in it for many years. They would go for months without ever seeing each other. At some point, one of the brothers died in his bed, and was not discovered for almost a year, when the smell got unbearable. Apparently, even the low price could not overcome the dead brother to make a sale possible, including us. We looked at a few more houses and even a small Inn in nearby Hagerstown, Maryland, but eventually gave up on moving off-site.

Growing Old in America

Health issues began to crop up that impacted my effectiveness as a full-time employee. When out "antiquing" one day, we stopped at a MacDonald's and I had my usual double cheeseburger, which usually resulted in a mild case of indigestion. By the time we got back to the Inn, I was experiencing chest pain severe enough to put me on the floor. I had this pain just underneath my breast bone from time to time, but never this severe. Sandy became alarmed that it might be a heart attack and whisked me down to the only doctor in town, the one who missed the diagnosis of the Inn's former owner's cancer. He poked me once in the stomach and announced "gall bladder", and said to get to the hospital immediately, as it had probably ruptured. He said to either call the local ambulance from the fire department or for Sandy to drive me. Remembering that the local ambulance crew had killed a man while performing CPR up at the ski resort who had only fainted, we opted to have Sandy drive me.

Sandy drove like a maniac, with horn blaring and in the turn only lane, some thirty miles up to the hospital in Chambersburg. I fell out of the suburban onto the lawn outside the Emergency Room and they carted me off to be admitted for surgery the next day. That night, Sandy came to see me and said we had a problem. The ER surgeon on call, who was to do the surgery, was seventy-five years old. We still had access to the physician national data base and she had checked him out. I called the Hospital Administrator and explained my situation and having held a similar position in my former life. He said he knew the surgeon was older, but if he, or any member of his family, required surgery this surgeon would do it. He ended the conversation by saying the surgeon was also his neighbor. Sandy and I talked it over and decided that the next surgeon on call could be "Doobie Howser", the sixteen-year-old surgeon from the TV sitcom. We went with experience!

The next morning came and I was in extreme discomfort from the fact they would not let me take my Hytrin pills because of the "nothing by mouth" pre-surgical orders. Unable to pee, my bladder was the size of a basketball and no amount of pleading with the nurses got me the pills. When placed on the operating table and just before the anesthesiologist placed the mask over my face, I asked him if it would be a problem if I pissed all over the operating table. I told him my predicament, and the last thing I remember was his shouting to "get a catheter in this guy, now!" The next morning, the surgeon, who flunked bedside manner 101 in medical school, stuck his head in the door and tossed a bag containing my gallstones at me, stating "see you in my office in two weeks." It was only later that I recalled a hallway consult, while working at Summit Medical Center, that resulted in an ultrasound of the kidney and gallbladder area, and a diagnosis of gall stones, which I had promptly ignored.

My other big medical problem occurred while restoring the sunken garden at 204 pounds during a 90 degree, 90 percent humidity Pennsylvania summer. I began having trouble getting up the stairs from the tiered garden and then up to the porch. I thought it was a touch of the flu and kept on working in the sunken gardens. When I could not make it up to the first floor from our basement apartment, Sandy insisted I see a cardiologist. I told her when she found an English speaking, American trained, board certified cardiologist I would go see him, or her. I thought I was safe from having to do that, as most physicians in the rural environ were both foreign trained and foreigners. Of course, Sandy found one in nearby Hagerstown, Maryland, and I make an appointment. Before even seeing the cardiologist, the staff did an EKG, and when the nurse rushed out of the room to get the doctor I knew I was in trouble. He said I was in some kind of rhythmic heart failure and to drive over to the hospital emergency room to be admitted to the hospital. This is where semantics entered the picture during future discussions with both Sandy and the cardiologist. My recollection was that he did not say to go to the ER NOW, but to just go. I had the dirty inn laundry to still deliver and my run to Costco in Virginia still to make, so when that was done I drove back to the Inn, unloaded the clean linen and supplies, and informed Sandy that she would have to drive me back to the hospital in Hagerstown to be admitted. She was not a happy camper, at this point!

By the time we got to the ER, I was not in good shape and they took me right in, bypassing all that registration crap. I went straight to the heart catheter lab and it was determined I had one heart artery blocked and needed a stent. That hospital was not authorized to do stents, so I was transferred by ambulance to St. Joseph's Regional Medical Center in Baltimore, where the PTCA (stent) was performed. The clearing of the blocked artery and insertion of the stent was performed by no other than, a Doctor Plaque. My cardiologist in Hagerstown was a piece of work. He was obese and smoked while seeing patients. When I told him Sandy had put me on the South Beach Diet, he said he was on the seafood diet himself. He saw food and ate it!

Sandy developed a frozen shoulder which she resolved with physical therapy and time, and I had a lens implant in my other eye, along with hernia surgery, to sum up medical problems while at the Inn. I still had my prostrate problem, my back put me out of commission from time to time, and the problem of "wooden toenails" plagued me from the second year at the Inn on. It started with one or two toes on each foot becoming discolored and then becoming crusty under the nail, which hardened and forced the nail up. The local General Practitioner said it was viral in nature and there were pills you could take for the problem. However, it would take six months for the pills to work, if at all, and the pills were horribly expensive. This was before I was Medicare eligible, so pills were not an option then, and I eventually put up with it even though the conditions spread to all the toes except the little ones. So much for medical problems while at the Inn.

By our fourth year of innkeeping, we began to think more seriously about an exit strategy. I had experienced my heart "episode", lost my gall bladder, and developed a hernia from working on restoring the sunken gardens on the lower tier of the property below the large porch. There were stone steps leading down to a brick path to the gardens that sat overgrown with weeds and the invasive roots of Paulownia Trees, or Royal Empress Trees, as they are sometimes called. These trees are amazing and very fast growing, sometimes fifteen feet in one year. They first emerge as a stick about eighteen inches tall and a week later it is a tree four feet tall. Mature trees grow large "elephant ear" branches and pods that turn into beautiful pink flowers. The bad feature of this tree is the root system, which is extremely invasive and destructive. The gardens were enclosed within thick brick walls that also served as dividers inside the garden. These brick walls were two to five foot high, depending on the tiered land, and were capped by three inch thick concrete slabs, five feet long by two feet wide. The invasive roots of the Paulownia Trees were instrumental in breaking down these walls, along with the help of neighborhood kids when the property sat abandoned. In the center of the gardens was a three-foot deep concrete reflecting pool, over which I built a trellis to replace one that had been destroyed. This was my project one hot and humid summer during which I pigged out on coca cola and ballooned up to 204 pounds.

The concrete slabs weighed a couple of hundred pounds and resulted in a hernia, and my added weight probably led to the heart problem, when I began to have problems with climbing the stairs back up to the porch. All this led up to our fourth anniversary at the Inn, in the year 2000, and a plan to spend the next millennium somewhere else, or at least a part of it somewhere else. Whatever plan we came up with would have to include our youngest daughter, Megan, who was then seventeen and with another year to go at the Academy. All senior students had to board at the school, which meant that the "plan" could be implemented any time after the school year started. Megan was an issue when we purchase the Inn and she was an issue when we decided to sell the Inn. I suppose any recollection of our innkeeping experience would have to include some mention of life with Megan.

RAISING A CHILD IN YOUR PLACE OF BUSINESS

When we first starting thinking about buying a Bed and Breakfast or Inn, and attended those seminars at the PAII annual meetings, there was always a session on "Raising your children at the facility". We both attended such sessions and came away with some do's and don'ts, but each situation is different, I suppose, and some things you just have to play by ear. Megan was fourteen the summer she came to the Inn and going to enter eighth grade at a public school, her first experience in the public school arena. She left behind two sisters and a brother, but had her dog and cat at the Inn. New town, new school, stuck with her parent's twenty-four/seven and in her early teens...a formula for disaster. But, she did well and got off to a great start. She made a tentative friend with the daughter of the local physicians, who had a horse on their property. That led to her association with the miniature horse people who later "adopted" her. The friend did not work out, but it broke the ice and she made some quick friends when school started. Megan did well in school academically and particularly in chemistry. She always complained about the chemistry teacher being too strict or the subject being too difficult, but when the term was up she went back to visit him a number of times. She did not participate in after-school activities that year, which was odd because back in California she had played basketball, was a flag-girl, and played the flute in band, orchestra, and the marching band.

Early on, Sandy decided Megan was going to get involved in the business, in some capacity, to earn money for her own personal wants and desires...horses were not cheap to maintain. Megan did not want any of the front-of-the-house jobs or doing wait-staff in the restaurant, so the only alternative was helping out in the kitchen. She preferred not dealing with the guests face-to-face, which was probably normal for a teenager. Sandy started her out in the dish room running the dish machine and she progressed to making salads and plating up food. She got along great with the three chefs we had over the years, and took care of the first chef's dogs, Bacon and Eggs, when he went away. By the time the second chef arrived, Megan was running the non-cooking side of the kitchen and this continued until her senior year at the Academy, when she had to live on campus.

Age fourteen and fifteen were difficult years for both mother and daughter, when the hormones were flowing in both directions for the respective parties. Megan would have nothing to do with Sandy, and Sandy was convinced that Megan had been switched at birth in the hospital and she was mothering a stranger. It all resolved itself almost overnight, at age sixteen, and they became best friends once again, to everyone's relief. Sixteen meant driving lessons from Dad and a decision by Mom to offer Megan her beloved 1984 Mercedes 380SL convertible. To our surprise, Megan turned her nose up at the Mercedes offer because it did not have a back seat or a CD player. What good was a car if you could not drive your friends around and listen to your music!

A car search followed and Megan settled on an older used Dodge two-door sedan with a back seat, but without a CD player. It was mechanically sound except for the driver door handle not working, which I thought I could fix, but found out later was unfixable. Megan did well with driving lessons and it soon came time for the driver's road test, which I thought would not be a problem for her. Unfortunately, some time had passed since driving lessons for her older siblings in another state, and she did not pass. She did pass the road driving part, but was unable to locate the flasher warning button on the dashboard, something I did not cover with her, nor even thought about covering. I felt bad about this oversight, and Megan was devastated. To admit failure to her friends of this simple "passage of independence" was unimaginable. I could remember how anxious her siblings had been over the driver's license test. Back when I was fifteen taking the test in a manual transmission and clutch car, one member of our "group" flunked the test and endured the ribbing of his classmates until graduation. Megan had to wait a month to retake the test, which she passed without any problems, but it was a long month of strained relationships at the Inn.

Growing Old in America

During the spring of her Junior Year at the Academy, Megan went to France with her French class and discovered that Parisians still do not like Americans. The adults at the home she stayed at would not speak to her or the other student with her. The son did converse without his parents present and other French people outside of Paris were very friendly, she reported. She liked Nice but decided she would not ever return to France. That summer she elected not to return to horse camp in Healdsburg, California, after five straight years and the last year as a counsellor.

Megan's senior year at the Academy arrived and she had to board across the street. Her other three years she was a day student and lived at home in the Inn. We ended up seeing more of Megan when she was boarding than when she lived at home with us. Day students were given a shared room to stay overnight in case there should there be late classes, or sports, inclement weather, or library time. She would stay over to visit with her friends, softball teammates, or occasional boyfriend. There was one particular boy she seemed interested in, over her last three years at the Academy, whom we were not too excited about. He was kind of a problem student who was threatened with expulsion a number of times. He was from a wealthy family in Florida and at the end of her junior year, they invited Megan to join them surfing in Costa Rica, which they did every summer. She decided that was too far away to be with a family she had never met and declined the offer before we had the opportunity to object.

Drugs were becoming a huge problem with teenage high school and college kids and the Academy had a zero tolerance policy that extended down to smoking and alcohol. Automatic expulsion and forfeiture of tuition was the penalty, which did not prove to be a deterrent, as several students left the campus each year for infractions of the policy. Megan made the right choices in choosing friends and avoiding hazardous situations, as far as we knew. She did not smoke, but did join her friends that went down to the pizza joint to do so. Her one indiscretion, which

I was unaware of for many years, was a belly button piercing. Sandy knew about it and kept it from me until Megan was on her own financially. I was not a fan of tattoos or piercings.

High School Graduation came in June of 2001. Always a big deal, it became bigger at the Academy. The big issue for Megan was that it came in 2001 instead of 2000, the year of the new millennium. Had we not made her repeat first grade, she would have graduated in 2000. We heard that sad story over and over before and after graduation. I almost had her convinced toward the end of 1999 that graduating in 2000 was problematic because of the pending Y2K computer virus that threatened universal computer crashing at the stroke of midnight on the 1999 New Year's Eve. That theory evaporated when nothing happened, and the moaning and groaning continued.

Graduation at the Academy was done with maximum pomp and circumstance and a lot of tradition sprinkled in. They had been doing it that way for over a hundred years. We invited my two sisters, Sandy's Dad, and the three siblings, with their families, which complicated things since the Inn was always full and overflowing with Academy parents at graduation time. Megan insisted on invited her brother Scott, whom she was still very fond of at this time. Scott had left Mercersburg to return to California on not very cordial terms, but I extended the invitation and offered to pay his way. I gave him my credit card number to buy his airline ticket, but when he arrived he was accompanied by his girlfriend, courtesy of good old dad's credit card. This girl friend was cut from the same mold as "Bouncy" from Dana's wedding at the winery. We thought that mold had been destroyed after Bouncy, but were sadly mistaken. Megan has since diagnosed the new girlfriend as bi-polar and we suffered through her stages of depression and euphoria for the long week-end. I told Scott that he would have to reimburse me for the girlfriend's airline ticket, and he reluctantly wrote me a check, which bounced for insufficient funds, of course.

Megan had been accepted at University of California, Santa Cruz, and decided to attend summer school out there to get some early credits and grease the skids for transferring up to the University of California, Davis for Veterinary School. It was decided that I would drive her out to California with her "stuff," in the Suburban, and stay with her until she could get into her student apartment for the fall semester. My college roommate, Eli, had inherited his recently deceased aunt's house in Campbell, on the San Francisco Peninsula only thirty minutes from the Santa Cruz campus, and let Megan and I stay there for the 8-10 weeks before the fall semester began. I kept the yard in shape and agreed to purchase some of the furnishings for Megan's college apartment. Megan found a job at a sunglass store in one of the numerous malls to keep her busy when not in her summer college class at Santa Cruz. We had purchased Sandy's fathers 1986 Cadillac, which had only 84,000 miles on it, a few years earlier and kept it in Santa Maria at her brothers, so when we flew out to California we would have a car. Sandy's dad drove the car up to us so that Megan would have wheels to get around in and I drove him home, stopping off on the way back to visit friends. Sandy and I then changed places, with her flying out to stay with Megan and me driving back to Mercersburg.

Sandy stayed with Megan during August and I flew out the first week in September and we all attended one of my college roommate's daughter's wedding. Sandy and I again changed places with her returning to the Inn and me staying with Megan until school started. During this time I had the occasion to visit with Scott and confronted him about the bad check issue. We have not spoken since that day.

One morning I got up and turned the TV on while eating a late breakfast and saw this unbelievably realistic movie about airplanes crashing into skyscrapers. A plane had crashed into the Empire State Building many years prior and, at first, I thought this to be a movie about the crash. The date that morning was September 11, 2001 and it was not a Hollywood movie I was watching. I called Sandy and found out a third plane had crashed in a field not too far from the Inn, on its way back to the White House. The Inn was directly in its flight path to the White House, it turned out. The next few days were hectic for Megan and I, and everyone else in America. I got Megan into her apartment with three other girls and drove down to Los Angeles Airport for the flight home. The airport was a fortified camp, with roadblocks and checkpoints everywhere. The terminal itself was almost empty and I was the first one to arrive at the gate. I found myself scrutinizing closely each new passenger as they checked in and you better believe I was ethnic profiling. And, wouldn't you know it, two bearded Arabic gentlemen showed up with carry-on luggage and I panicked. The airline had this device above the check-in counter that showed the seat that each passenger checked in to, on a display of the plane's interior. These two guys had separate seats at opposite ends of the cabin, and I almost took a later flight.

When I got back to the Inn, I found out that my IBM son-in-law, Kevin, had been in Manhattan on 9-11 and ran out of the City on foot, found a car rental place, and drove non-stop to Peachtree City in Georgia. Overnight, we lost all the business person business as all business-related travel stopped. It took a while before the normal leisure travel business returned, except for weekenders out of the big cities, possibly seeking to escape the next target zone.

Megan completed her freshman year at UC Santa Cruz and transferred to Emory University in Atlanta, Georgia. She still had an interest in Veterinary Medicine, but gave up on California education. In her second semester at San Cruz, she was called in to the English Department Dean's office and questioned about what English honors classes she had taken or what tutoring she had the benefit of. They were amazed when she told them she had just taken the regular English classes at the Academy. What she did not tell them was every paper written at the Academy got graded twice, once by the course being taking and again by the English Department. The Dean admitted to Megan that she was an anomaly because many California students could not write a simple sentence or read with comprehension. Megan said UC Santa Cruz was not a "learning environment" and I threatened to have her DNA tested to see if she really was a Filkowski. Being a "football" school or a "beach" school or "party" school were acceptable criteria for colleges, but a "learning environment" was not in my DNA.

Megan transferred into Emory University for her sophomore year in the fall of 2002 along with her pet goldfish. This goldfish travelled west with us in the suburban the previous summer I drove her out to California. It made it through that summer in Campbell, the two semesters at U.C. Santa Cruz, the following summer at Sandy's ex-husband's house in Aptos, California, and a road trip back to Mercersburg with Sandy's father late that same summer. She drove the goldfish down to Atlanta and it lived with her in a small dorm room. That goldfish had more road miles on it than most people do in a lifetime.

Her older Dodge sedan began to feel the mileage on it, and on a Christmas drive home to Mercersburg it suffered a rear axle separation. She had to spend overnight in a small-town motel by herself until I could come get her the next day. Her roommate had cancelled out on driving home with her and the situation upset her more than she admitted. We ended up replacing the Dodge with a newer Volkswagen our payroll guy was selling, for her return trip to Atlanta. Merry Christmas!

Megan's other early traumatic Emory experience was her Organic Chemistry Class. Because she was still in a pre-veterinary tract, she had to take the same Organic Chemistry class that pre-med students took, and both she and her roommate were getting "F"s in the class. I was in the same situation at SF State in a Physics class and assured her that they graded on a curve and most of the class were probably failing; which meant she would get at least a "C". I was wrong and she got an "F"; her first failing grade ever. She actually went into a mild depression and I felt terrible; until I found out years later that the two roommates had been out to the clubs a bit too much that semester, and experimented with the drug Ecstasy.

To become a Veterinarian, one must work, not volunteer, in a Veterinarian Office/Clinic for a year before being admitted to a

Veterinary School. Megan did her year part-time and became disillusioned with the business techniques she witnessed in the profession. She switched majors to Psychology her junior year.

FINAL DAYS

At the end of the 2001 school year at the Academy, after Megan had graduated, the current Student Body President, at the urging of the Senior Class, petitioned the school to allow a senior class trip before graduation. I was surprised to learn this was not already the custom, but remembered that Megan had not experienced this the year before. The Academy not only said no, they said "hell no." This would be a first, and for a school so steeped in tradition, it was unthinkable. I am sure there were liability issues to consider, but the senior class persisted and the student body leadership eventually prevailed. The school allowed a senior class camping trip up in northwest Pennsylvania east of the Penn State Campus, with faculty chaperones, no smoking, and no alcohol or drugs... yeah sure!

The entire senior class left to go camping and everyone held their breath. If anything went wrong, it would prove to be the first and last senior trip. On the second or third night, a tornado ripped through the area barely missing their camp site, but wiping out a nearby town. The school and parents panicked, but soon learned that the entire class pitched in and spent the remainder of their week helping the townspeople clean up from the devastating tornado. It was an experience those kids will never forget and a lesson they would never have learned in a classroom. There have been senior trips ever since, as far as I know!

The class of 2001 thanked the Academy by pulling off a graduating class prank that proved to be the best to date. They erected a large FOR SALE sign at the main entrance to the campus off highway 16 the night before graduation, and the school actually received a few inquiries before taking down the sign. This prank outshone Megan's senior class prank the year before where they applied clear shrink wrap over the toilets, but under the seats, throughout the campus except in a few places for their own use.

Meanwhile, back at the Inn, the handwriting was on the wall by the "Fire Alarm Wedding Incident", as it later became known. During one of Sandy's big production weddings at the Inn, the fire alarm went off right before the grand entrance of the bride down the double curved wrought iron balustrade staircase into the grand foyer. I raced down to the fire alarm master display in the mechanical room to find out the location of the fire and raced up the four flights of stairs in the back hallway to the third floor where the alarm had been pulled. I found the mother of the bride holding a two-year old with the glass rod from the fire alarm in his grubby little hand. "Wasn't that cute", she stated, "he just wanted to see what would happen when he pulled it." I told her, in no uncertain terms, what would happen to her and to him if it happened again. There was some disagreement later on about my exact phraseology, but the damage was done by that time. This all came about after a fairly recent incident where I had told an obnoxious dinner guest that "if he did not like it, he should go elsewhere."

Thereafter, I was relegated to parking cars during weddings and other large events, and I was monitored by wait-staff during my interactions with dinner guests. It was during one of my car parking stints that a man drove up and introduced himself as my nephew, my brother's son. We had never met and, unfortunately, a wedding was in progress, the Inn was totally booked, and I was busy parking cars. He was passing through on his way somewhere and he left. I always felt bad about how that went down, but did not know what else to do.

Again, it was during the final year at the Inn that we decided to remodel the carriage house and use it as an "owner's residence." We were in a position financially to do it, although it went over-budget considerably after we decided to make it possible to use as guest rooms as well. Sandy's Dad had drawn up plans a few years earlier and we used those with some modifications.

We had begun running ads about selling the Inn in 2000 and had some interest early on, but always from novice innkeepers that wanted us to carry the financing. We wanted an "all cash" deal or nothing at all. The last thing we wanted was to take the Inn back after new owners had failed to make a go of it or ran it into the ground. We got within five weeks of a deal in February of 2001, but the buyer could not get financing. We decided to use an on-line Inn Real Estate service that was run by people we knew from our Inn Association. They dealt exclusively with high-end properties and charged a hefty fee, but seemed to get results. They had an excellent web site that shortened the buy/sell experience greatly from the time we were looking back in the early 1990's.

When I called these people to inquire about using their services, I was told that they had looked at our property back in 1996 when the former owner wanted to list it, and it was not upscale enough for them. I convinced them to take another look which they did, and took our listing. The listing got a lot of play, but the service stopped there and we ended up doing all the showings and leg work. We did get a buyer finally that was financially qualified, but with no experience in innkeeping. They disliked the listing service people and would only deal with us, which was not what we paid for, but we had a buyer and wanted out by this time.

Closing was set for March originally, but got pushed back to May of 2004. The price was close to our asking and it was a turn-key deal with a few exceptions, namely the piano, and some family related items. I left the big grandfather clock because I did not want to pack it up, and have regretted that decision. The buyers also purchased the 1996 Suburban and snow plow and all inventory, including liquor, linens, food, and gift shop…a statistical nightmare. Closing was stressful because the owner of the listing service insisted on being present to collect the balance of his exorbitant commission, but the new owners did not want him present. Our attorney finally assured him he would get his money, and we closed without him in the room.

Meanwhile, we had to find a place to go. We had ruled out

returning to California because of real estate values and the cost of living. My daughter Dana had undergone In Vitro twice to get pregnant, and had twin boys on the second attempt in December, 2003. We still had the cabin up near Yosemite and that made two good reasons to go back, but retired seniors did not do well in California. Megan was still at Emory down in Atlanta and Sandy's daughter Lauri and her family, now at four with the addition of Andrew in 1997, were in Peachtree City, just south of Atlanta. On one of our Christmas trips down to Lauri's, we looked at the North Carolina Mountains, particularly Hiawassee. The town sat on a lake and had a small hospital, where sandy might have found an accounting job, even a CFO position. Sandy has decided that she would have to work until she hit Social Security age, but what she really wanted was not to be stuck around me all day. Hiawassee was about two and one half hours from Atlanta and Lauri's family which was close enough for me, but not close enough for Sandy. She wanted more access to the two grandkids, which were then in the eight to ten year old age bracket.

Sandy subscribed to COOKING LIGHT MAGAZINE for a long time in an attempt to keep my weight down, and found a COOKING LIGHT house design located in a place called "Big Canoe," one hour north of Atlanta, Georgia, that she liked. Over Christmas week in 2003, we went to Lauri's house in Peachtree City, and on one of those days I drove up to Big Canoe to see what was going on. I bluffed my way through the main manned gate, and drove into the 8000 acre mountain community through the covered bridge and was hooked. On the way back to Mercersburg from Lauri's with Sandy aboard, we bluffed our way through the gate again and drove through the covered bridge and Sandy was hooked. On subsequent visits to Big Canoe with a realtor and Megan along, we purchased a newly constructed house. Neither of us had ever owned a brand new house before, so this was going to be a new experience for us. We liked new experiences! It was a three bedroom, 3400 square foot house on two levels, a main level and a garden level. It had two master suites, one on each level, which Sandy wanted because she planned on having her father move out from California to live with us. She also liked the kitchen, which is an important point to remember later on. During a subsequent trip to the Atlanta area, we purchased a low-mileage 2001 Lexus 430LS, the big four-door sedan and the best car I ever owned. Thus, we renewed our preference for not buying new cars and eating the depreciation the day we drove it off the dealer's lot. We left Sandy's 1984 Mercedes 380sl convertible at Lauri's house in Peachtree City and drove back up to the Inn to complete our one month of orientation for the new owners.

The new owners owned three condos in Manhattan and sold one of them to buy the Inn from us. They knew less than we did about innkeeping when we started out and needed a lot of orientation. However, they spent every weekend of the orientation month back in Manhattan, in spite of innkeeping being primarily a weekend business. The husband planned on doing breakfast for the guests as Sandy was doing, but little training transpired since most of it would have happened on the weekends. The same went for almost all other aspects of the operation except for the computer and bookkeeping, which they could pick up on during the week. As the end of the month approached, we made it abundantly clear we would be gone as planned. We also let it be known to staff and the new owners that we would be headed to our cabin in California, after attending the twins christening, after dropping off our stuff at the new house in Big Canoe.

Since we would not be taking much in the way of furniture, we decided to rent a truck and drive it down to Big Canoe ourselves. We had done that when bringing out some furniture back in 1994, but were eight years younger and in better health back then. We opted to hire a crew to load the truck at the Inn and another crew to offload at the new house. I found a temp agency, in nearby Chambersburg, to provide us an experienced moving crew and we commenced packing up our "stuff." We also hired a piano moving crew to pack up the piano, but I elected not to take our big grandfather clock, a big mistake on my part. Our "stuff" turned out to begin outgrowing the largest U-Haul truck they rented, and the Lexus was going to have to handle the overflow. Our exit preparations were continuously being interrupted by local friends and vendors dropping in to say good-by, so we decided to throw a "going-away party," and timed it for mid-week when the new owners would be present and make it also a "meet the new owners" affair. We were surprised by the turnout and the genuine sadness expressed at seeing us leave the Inn, mostly for Sandy's leaving I have to admit.

With our good-byes behind us, moving day arrived and, of course, it rained cats and dogs. After waiting an hour past the time they were supposed to arrive, I called the temp service to find out where our moving crew was. They informed me a message had been left at the Inn a couple of days previously about the crew being hired for a more lucrative move in Chambersburg. They did not remember who took the message, but there were some men hanging around their office waiting for jobs to open up and they would send them out to us at ten dollars per hour. I could not imagine who took such a message and did not pass it on, unless it was someone that did not want us to leave right away. It took all I had not to bite my tongue clear through, but I told them to send out four men ASAP.

Three derelicts, right off the street, arrived two hours later. The fourth decided en-route that he needed a drink, and never did show up. I put them to work right away loading the truck because I was now being "encouraged" by the new owners to be gone as soon as possible, so they could move into the carriage house. This was news to us and made me wonder if they had overheard my ranting and raving about who had taking the message from the temp agency. Later on we learned they never did move into the carriage house, but made it guest accommodations instead. Our "crew" required constant supervision, but the truck and Lexus were finally loaded and ready to go by three o'clock. The Lexus was crammed except for the driver's seat, and some items had to be stuffed behind the seats in the truck, which proved to be a bad idea.

We left the Inn parking lot and Mercersburg in heavy rain, with me driving the truck and Sandy driving the Lexus. Charlie, the cat, rode with me in the truck perched up on the dashboard beneath the windshield, his usual spot. After a few hours, however, he ended up under the driver's seat and remained there until we arrived at Big Canoe. The trip down on highway 81 was slow due to the rain, steep hills, and truck traffic. I would slow down to 35 miles per hour on the hills with the gas pedal pushed to the floor. We arrived in Big Canoe almost twelve hours later and I was exhausted from manhandling that truck. We entered through the north gate, made three right hand turns onto our street, and preceded down to our new house where I turned the big U-Haul into the driveway and "crash," putting the double set of right rear wheels into a drainage culvert.

We were too tired to do anything except drag out a mattress and fall asleep in our new house. The next morning I called the builder and he arranged for the biggest tow truck, the one that hauls away eighteen wheelers, to come haul us out of the drainage culvert. The tow truck driver offered to back the U-Haul down into our driveway and a crew arrived to off-load under Sandy's supervision. The cost for the tow truck was commensurate with the size of the truck. The next day we piled into the Lexus and drove off to California for the twins Baptism. To make it on time for the Baptism, we drove the 2500 miles in two and a half days, a feat we would repeat in each of the next twelve years, with few exceptions. We were pleasantly surprised with the Baptism because all of our kids had dropped religion as a priority after leaving home, but both girls had their kids Baptized. Lauri's family actually had a brief "all-in" experience with religion when their boys were small, but something happened and they ended up becoming atheists. Dana continued attending services sporadically, and then more frequently as her twins got older. I credit this to Sandy's influence during Dana's part-time with us during her teenage years.

We spent almost two months in California that first summer after leaving the Inn, seeing friends and family, and spending time at the cabin fixing up things neglected over the years at the Inn. Upon our return to Big Canoe, we found the house to be in better shape than we left it because Lauri and Megan had come up and unpacked what they could and set up our king size bed for us to fall into after the extended road trip.

Walt Filkowski

LIFE IN BIG CANOE

We started life in Big Canoe with me just turning 65 and eligible for Social Security and Medicare. None too soon, as it turned out. We spent a few months unpacking and buying new furniture for our first-ever brand new house, and soon discovered new is not always best. We found out the independent builder had some financial problems after his partner ran off with their money, and he had to make a deal with the Developer to help finish the house. The deal apparently involved listing and selling the house, among other things. What we did not know, when looking for a house in Big Canoe, was that the developer owned the onsite real estate company. This meant that when you used this realtor you were only shown homes the Developer built or controlled. So, our final walkthrough on the punch list was conducted by an employee of the developer.

There were several other builders and real estate companies active in the development that we were not aware of. "FOR SALE" signs were not allowed on properties and only realtors knew what homes and lots were for sale. It turned out that the agent we were assigned to by Big Canoe Realty had just started working there and we were his first sale. The major issue with the quality of the house was the spacing and finish on the hardwood floors. The builder claimed the Georgia Building Code allowed for up to a quarter of an inch space between hardwood floor boards, which is outright ridiculous. We did get the floors refinished after showing the builder how a swifter sheet could not pass over the floors without snagging. Unfortunately, he had the same people do the refinishing and the result was the same. We learned much later from neighbors, that the floors were laid just before a rainstorm and windows and doors had not been installed.

Other things we were not informed of included the fact a tornado had passed through Big Canoe four years earlier with considerable damage, the land behind our ¾ acre lot could be developed (our agent told us the opposite), and that motorcycles were not allowed inside the gates. This last one was particularly galling since our agent asked me what I was going to do as a new resident, and when I replied that I planned to buy a motorcycle he volunteered that another resident had just won a Harley Davidson and did not ride. He inferred that the bike was probably up for sale at a good price. There was no mention of motorcycles not being allowed in the development.

Big Canoe had a leash law for dogs, which served a dual purpose of protecting residents from loose dogs and also protecting the dogs from coyotes, bear, and wild boar that roamed the area. Outdoor cats were discouraged for obvious reasons, but no mention was made of packs of dogs from neighbors living adjacent to the Big Canoe development. Charlie, the big white cat that adopted us our last year at the Inn, was an outdoor cat and paid the price by being killed by such a pack of dogs.

After some initial "settling in," Sandy began looking for a job. At the same time, she was asked to model in a community fashion show at the tender age of 56. She was still pretty good looking at fifty-six, and was a hit at the show. Sandy felt it necessary to work until Social Security eligible, a time that was becoming less and less known, as the Federal Government discussed pushing eligibility dates past sixty-five. During her search for a job, the General Manager position for the Big Canoe Property Owners Association came open, and she applied for that $150,000 position. The search firm gentleman that interviewed her made it quite clear, without coming out and saying it, that it was a man's job. He then made a gigantic boo-boo and asked Sandy her age, and upon hearing 56, said she was too old. She could have made an issue out of it, but she did not, because that is not her way. She found another position as Chief Financial Officer of the nearby State Park at Amicalola Falls, for considerably less money.

The state park system in Georgia is quite extensive and very well done. Some of them include golf courses, which often rivaled the private courses. Amicalola State Park was only fifteen minutes from our house and included a very tall water floor dropping down from the top of a mountain. At the top was also a lodge with rooms, a restaurant, the administrative offices, and a network of hiking trails. One of the trails connected to the "Appalachian Trail," a trail that traveled up the East Coast as far as Maine. Another trail terminated after five miles at another, more rustic lodge. They had a "hike in" package that included hiking in to this lodge, staying overnight with a family style dinner, and hiking back out the next morning. It was very popular and required reservations weeks in advance. We always talked about doing it, but never could pull it off. At the bottom of the mountain were a museum, gift shop, park ranger programs, and a petting zoo. Sometimes I would ride my motorcycle up the winding road to the top and have lunch with the new Chief Financial Officer.

Sandy did very well in her short tenure at the park, and hit the road running as she usually did. She reorganized the office and was soon the confident of the Chief Operating Officer of the whole operation. Unfortunately for the Park System, it was policy to have the person in charge be a park ranger. Finance, food service, and hotel accommodations were not included in the Park Range school curriculum. Soon they wanted Sandy to take over the lodge and restaurant operation along with finance, but she declined because everything would have had to be approved by both her Park Ranger boss and the Park System. After attending a regional meeting down at one of the parks in Southern Georgia, there was talk of bringing her into the regional office to head up finance for the entire system. I attended the meeting as a spouse and got in a lot of golf on a really nice course for twelve dollars for eighteen holes.

About this time, the park ranger COO found himself in hot water when it was discovered he had ordered the burial of asbestos laden material, collected from a recent lodge remodeling project, on park property. Definitely a no-no for a conservation-oriented organization, especially when the press got wind of it. This would have been perfect timing for Sandy to step in and take over, but she was not a park ranger, case closed! Instead they appointed the park ranger woman running the lodge to be interim COO, and put "Peter's Principle" into effect. This poor woman had trouble just running the lodge portion of the operation.

Also, about this time, the newly appointed General Manager for Big Canoe began a search for a new Director of Finance. He had retired after twenty-five years as City Manager of a small town in middle Kansas, a fact that seemed to escape the search committee of the Property Owners Board. They viewed Big Canoe as a small city since it had police, fire, water/sewer, parks, taxation/revenue, recreation, and public works services already in place. What they chose to ignore was the word "retired" in his resume. Sandy applied for this position because it provided better pay and benefits, was even closer to home than the state park, and her current job was becoming somewhat tenuous. She interviewed for the position and it came down to her and the interim Director. In fact, she had multiple interviews and it seemed the new General Manager had a problem with making decisions. Sandy finally had to tell him to _ _ _t or get off the pot, or she was going to pursue opportunities at the Park System. That apparently got his attention and he chose her to be his financial wizard, which as it turned out, became the case.

Walt Filkowski

WHAT WAS A BIG CANOE?

The history of Big Canoe can be found in a book titled "Wolf Scratch Wilderness", and written by Charlene Terrell, a long-term Big Canoe Resident. For us, who moved there in the summer of 2004, it was an 8000 acre gated mountain community with seven mountains, 100 miles of paved roads; three lakes with a 110 slip marina, beach, and in-ground water slide, three nine hole golf courses, fitness center with a pool and indoor tennis courts, outdoor tennis courts, bocce ball courts, 15 miles of hiking trails, an outdoor amphitheater, its own cemetery, a chapel and conference center, three fire stations inside the gates and one outside the gates with EMT's and ambulance service, two staffed entrance gates, a storage yard for resident motor homes and boats, outdoor basketball court, dog park, maintenance yard with offices, lodge on one of the lakes for events and meetings, and a clubhouse/restaurant that also served as the golf shop. Another outdoor pool complex and dog park was added after we arrived. There was also a commercial complex in the middle of the development owned by the developer that housed his real estate office, a wedding /convention center, shops, restaurant, and parking area. The complex was planned for 4750 lots, and already had about 2500 homes built and occupied and another 750 lots sold. In addition to the developer, any approved builder could build in Big Canoe. Some builders purchased lots and built their spec homes, with design approval of course. The developer built, and sold off, condos and townhomes which became time-share communities with their own assessments and fees, in addition to the Big Canoe assessments.

There were some negatives with all the positives, as was to be expected. There were lots of amenities, but they were ala carte, and they were not inexpensive. The only freebee was the clubhouse, which housed the bar and restaurant and was built in the 1970's. The roads were all paved, but windy and narrow up and down mountainous terrain without streetlights or sidewalks. Trash and garbage had to be hauled to a central location inside the gates, and was a considerable distance for most residents. Mail and packages were also delivered to a single location and you had to pick them up from your private box. For Sale signs were not allowed on the property and the only way to sell your home or lot was through a realtor. Covenants were very strict, particularly as related to landscaping and construction/remodeling projects. This last item was both good and bad, as it kept home and lot values high. Big Canoe was also pretty isolated from the rest of the world, and that became an issue when the community began to age. An IGA grocery chain had only recently opened nearby some two or three years earlier, along with a couple of marginal restaurants, but the closest town was thirty miles from the South gate on a windy road and even longer for residents on top of the mountains. A minor negative was the propensity for tornados to come through the area every ten years, with the last one arriving just behind our new house four years previously.

A last negative, when we moved there in 2004, was that the Developer still had control of the community. Later, when the residents took over control, there was a feeling of "be careful what you wish for", because the Developer had done a pretty good job of maintaining his vision of being the best mountain community in Georgia. He made some business decisions that offended some residents, but after all, he did own the place. And, as fate would have it later on, the residents made some dumb decisions when they were in a position to do so. The Developer included in his vision that the community would be multi-generational and include young families. That was always going to be a tough row to hoe with schools 45 minutes away, no childcare, and kids having to be driven everywhere they went, no sidewalks, and no streetlights. A lot of the Developer implemented amenities were child-oriented, which turned out to be o.k. for grand-kids, but went unused by the fewer that ten per cent of under-eighteen residents.

So, this was Big Canoe when we were moved in and settled, by the fall of 2004. We really liked the mountain atmosphere, and the residents turned out to be mostly seniors. Sandy took the Director of Finance/CFO position for the Big Canoe Property Owners Association, known as the POA, for twice her salary at the State Park. I was now left alone all day at home and became Mr. Mom. Friday became laundry and house cleaning day and dinner was ready when Sandy got home on most Monday through Thursday nights. I became proficient at five basic meals, in addition to spaghetti. Meatloaf, balsamic chicken, salmon, Joe's Special, and tomato basil mozzarella soup, rounded out my culinary acumen. We went out for Pizza or Chinese on Friday or a weekend night. Sandy cooked and baked on the weekends and cleaned anything that she thought I had been deficient in cleaning during the week.

I was determined to keep off the forty pounds I lost following my heart episodes and the subsequent South Beach Diet Sandy put me on. A few pounds had returned, but the trip to California that first summer after we left the Inn took care of those. Raking and burning an acre of pine straw will do that. In addition to walking, riding my motorcycle, and playing golf, I began swimming laps at the fitness center. My new cardiologist cautioned me about doing too much, but I felt good and continued my routine. Finding new physicians and a dentist for Sandy and I had not proven too difficult, but the distances we had to travel were annoying. Word of mouth proved to be the best way of finding medical services. I played golf with a neighbor two houses up the street and eventually was invited to fill in a foursome, when one of the golfers died. That turned out to be my entrée to a lot of social situations. I was subbing in a poker game and became a permanent member upon the death of player. Playing golf with my neighbor led to my participating in a weekly nine-hole senior players group, the Fossils. When the founder and manager of that group died, they renamed the group after his initials, and it became the ACE's. Death turned out to be almost a monthly, and sometimes weekly, occurrence in Big Canoe, as we got to know more and more residents.

We lived on Cherokee Way in the Cherokee neighborhood of Big Canoe. There were nine distinct separate such neighborhoods inside the gates. Geographically, we were comprised of two main streets, Cherokee Way and Cherokee Drive; with a short appendage off each,

Cherokee Point and Cherokee Knoll. All streets in our neighborhood ended in a cul de sac. There were thirty-two lots, of ¾ to one acre each, with 26 occupied homes, including ours, when we moved in. Within two years, there were 32 occupied homes. This neighborhood was eerily similar to a neighborhood we move into much later. A friendly neighbor (I played golf with the husband), befriended us and introduced us around to the other residents on our street. She introduced Sandy to making sourdough cinnamon bread from a starter, and Sandy has been making it almost weekly ever since. They also introduced us to the domino game, Mexican Train, and we were invited to play in a monthly game with four neighbor couples from our street. One of the couples lived half way down the hill that our street ended on, and the husband had trouble walking up that half of the hill, which he blamed on the flu; sound familiar? His wife could not get him to see a cardiologist, but he promised to do so when they returned from vacation. While on vacation at a resort up north, he walked out of their cabin one morning and dropped dead. We had not known them very long, but had we known his medical problem would have advised him see the cardiologist immediately.

We reinstituted our annual Christmas party that first holiday season in Big Canoe, and invited our street and the people Sandy worked with. We have had a holiday party every year since. Some years we also had a New Year's party, but on a smaller scale. Let's face it, we liked to party! Having a party results in getting invited to parties, and we got to know a lot more people in Big Canoe, especially our neighbors. As already mentioned, there were not many kids inside the gates, but we had as many as seven in the Cherokee neighborhood, and three on our street. The house on one side of us had two young boys, about eight and ten years old, and they were the most polite kids you could ever find. We were Miss Sandy and Mr. Walt, and we enjoyed them a lot. Sandy would bake them goodies and they always got our leftover Halloween candy. They had a friend up the street their age who had been adopted from an orphanage in Russia. Two other sets of kids lived across from each other on the other main Cherokee street, but moved away during the 2007- 2012 economic downturn. Their parents were real estate agents working for the Developer and real estate went in the tank big time in Big Canoe. They were replaced by a new set of twins, and then an unexpected third, by a young couple that moved onto our street during the end of the economic downturn.

Since I was home during the week, I got to know the neighbors better sooner than Sandy, because even the working residents mostly worked at home. One neighbor man was one year older than me; otherwise I was the oldest on the street, and probably one of the oldest in the Cherokee neighborhood. Walking the dog up and down the street three times a day usually put me in contact with the other dog owners in the area on a daily basis. There were nine other dogs living in the thirteen homes on our street when we moved in. When we moved away, there were four, including ours, in the fifteen houses then on the street. Pet longevity was not a big factor in the Cherokee neighborhood.

We moved to Big Canoe with only Charlie, the cat who thought he was a dog. Sheba, our German Shephard Inn dog, had been put down from old age during those last years at the Inn, and we vowed not to have another dog because of that trauma and our plans to travel. Megan had bestowed a couple of cats on us during her college days, but we were not going to allow the "kid's pets syndrome" to occur at Big Canoe. There was actually an enforced leash law and a limit of one cat and one dog in place, to assist in our own policy. Around that first Christmas in Big Canoe, Megan paid us a visit with her new acquisition, a Chihuahua puppy small enough to carry around in her purse. She had acquired the puppy from the veterinarian office she was working at part-time. The puppy's owner did not want it anymore and sold it to Megan for a very reasonable price. The puppy was very small and almost looked like a "teacup" type, but Megan assured us it was an "apple head" and would grow to a full size Chihuahua. Megan asked if we would babysit the dog for a week while she went skiing over her semester break from Emory. Sandy could not resist the chance to mother something, and the hook was set.

A couple of weeks after the "sitting" hook was placed; Megan decided she could not keep the dog in her "no pets allowed" apartment, because of his persistent barking. She already had two cats in the apartment and did not want to risk losing them. So guess who wound up with the dog and all his paraphernalia, including his litter box. The puppy grew up with cats and learned to do his business in their litter box. That proved to be a definite plus on cold winter nights, when all I had to do was put him in the laundry room to do his business. "Oliver", our new house guest, was o.k. with Charlie, because he had been "catanized" at Megan's apartment. Charlie was o.k. with Oliver, up to a point, but then one swipe off his claws across Oliver's face ended involvement for a while. We ended up with a cat that thought he was a dog, and a dog that was raised to be a cat.

Not too long after settling in at the new house, I developed lower back pain across my lower back and increased difficulty in urinating, that was different from the usual periodic back strain or vertebral nerve pain I was accustomed to. I put up with it for a while, thinking it would eventually go away, but the discomfort increased daily until, finally, I had enough and headed for the Emergency Room Of course, this occurred on a Sunday night and the ER was packed. My medical emergencies always seemed to occur on a weekend, for some reason. I waited two hours and finally just left for home, where I proceeded to take every pain medication I could find in the medicine cabinet. In our search for new physicians after the move to Big Canoe, the urologist in the nearby town of Jasper was recommended and I called for an appointment the following day. When I described my symptoms to the clerk, she told me to come in right away and they would squeeze me in.

Squeezing me in meant completing a ton of paper work and peeing in a cup, but I was eventually seen by a nurse and then, very quickly, by the urologist. Once again I heard the familiar cry of "get a catheter in this guy", and some minutes later they had collected 2000 ccs from my bladder. The urologist said the bladder can normally hold 80 ccs of urine before it backs up into the kidneys. He said I was probably about an hour away from that happening. While the kidneys produce urine initially, if it flows back to the kidney it will kill the tissue and the kidney, and dialysis would become necessary. I had dodged a major bullet, but was not out of the woods yet. My bladder collapsed when emptied, and I would have to wear a bag and catheter until it inflated again, if ever. I wore the apparatus for three weeks that included a driving trip up to New York for my oldest sister's 50th wedding anniversary celebration. Needless to say, there was not much dancing at the celebration, on my part.

Apparently, my beach ball sized prostrate had just about closed off the vessel that empties the bladder, and a surgical procedure would be necessary to rectify the situation. There was not any indication of cancer cells present, so total removal of the prostate was not indicated. The procedure of choice (not mine) was what every male fears, the TURP, or transurethral resection of the prostate. In layman terms, it is the rotor router job up through the penis to remove part of the prostate from the inside. To complicate matters, the increased straining associated with attempting to urinate through a much narrowed urethra had produced another hernia which would require surgery. It was decided to have both surgeries done at the same time, with a general surgeon doing the hernia repair and the urologist doing the TURP. I imagined they flipped a coin to see who operated first, but it did not matter to me. Sandy told me that the urologist told her in the waiting room that he had never had to take out so much tissue from a prostate. I could vouch for that because when I woke up, it felt like he had driven a dump truck up my penis to haul the tissue out. The second hernia repair went o.k., and that was the extent of my medical problems for some time. The urologist took me off the Hytrin and my new cardiologist took me off Plavix and eventually the blood thinner, Warfarin. I had once told my daughter, Dana the prosecutor, that I had a $400 a month drug habit. When she stopped yelling at me, I told her it was prescription medicines, and she calmed down.

Growing Old in America

MOTORCYCLE TIME

With my medical problems behind me, it was now time to pursue my search for a motorcycle. My preference was a Harley Davidson low rider, but even a used one proved to be out of my price range. I had ridden an older Kawasaki with Scott when I bought him his first dirt bike, and later stripped it down even further and took it up to the California cabin where it became the cabin bike. There was a Kawasaki dealership in Jasper and I was drawn to a bike there, but it too was out of my price range. The owner had built an Indian Chief Motorcycle replica from an 800cc 2004 Kawasaki that I could not resist. It was a bigger bike than I wanted, but it was a beauty. It had front and rear skirts on the wheels and the seat was converted to a leather saddle. The pipes were chromed and roared and rumbled, and everything else that could have been chromed, was. My last motorcycle had been a 150cc Honda street bike that I rode across the country back in 1979. The replica Indian was the bike I should have been riding on that trip. I ended up paying more than I wanted to even though the owner was motivated to sell the bike. He had just had hip replacement surgery and would never ride a big bike again, but he knew he had a winner in that particular bike.

Since motorcycles were not allowed inside the gates of Big Canoe, I had to rent a storage unit in the facility across the street from the North Gate. I could walk there from our house, so it was not that inconvenient. My neighbor, the Allstate Insurance agent, also ran the storage unit for the facility owner, who lived on the next street over from us. He needed a storage unit himself and we ended up sharing a unit. Our neighbor also ended up with our house and car insurance, and then the motorcycle insurance. When we moved down to Big Canoe, one of the first chores was to get insurance coverage on everything. I had State Farm Insurance coverage on everything I owned, including the sailboat and the cars at the Inn, for almost forty years, so we found a State Farm office in Jasper and signed us up. We soon found out that the State Farm rates were outrageously high, and when I called our State Farm agent back in Mercersburg to find out why, he said State Farm agents in Georgia make the most money of insurance agents anywhere else in the country. We switched over to Allstate and saved almost half the annual premiums we were paying, initially! Within a few years the rates crept up and we jumped to Progressive Insurance, where the rates dropped by half, initially! We played the game of low rates to get the business one more time until we found the military insurance, USAA, and even then the rates crept up, but the service was exceptional.

I had given up my motorcycle license when I applied for a new license in Pennsylvania, and Sandy and I had undergone the ordeal of getting a new Georgia driving license at the small DMV office in Canton. While waiting in a long line at the Canton office, we were told that the Blue Ridge office was huge and usually empty. We found this to be true and worth the long drive. I found out that a new DMV office had opened up just off highway 400 in Dawsonville, which was closer than driving up to Blue Ridge. When I presented myself at the motorcycle counter in Dawsonville, the man asked what I wanted and I replied that I wanted to get a motorcycle license. He said that I would not get one because I was too old, at age 65. When I commented that it was us "old people" who had the time and money to buy and ride motorcycles, he again said that I would not get a license there. I replied that we would see about that and to give me the application, which he did. He also said that he gave the riding test and could guarantee that I would not pass. I wished I had a tape recorder!

Test day came and I went a little early to observe the process. They had a tight driving course laid out just beyond the parking lot and I stood outside without the smokers to watch the driving test being given. I watched along with another older gentleman who was up next for the test. He said he was told the same thing by the tester, and had gone out and gotten motorcycle driving lessons just in case. He drove a smaller bike which, in retrospect I should have brought with me. I watched his test closely and he seemed to do O.K., but when he drove off I gave him a "thumbs up" and he replied with a "thumbs down." Now it was my turn and I was a little nervous. The tester's first comment to me was that it was against the rules for me to watch other riders being tested. I lied and said I was merely outside smoking with the smokers. He liked my Indian replica, but said it was too big a bike for me. I thought the test went alright and only crossed a line once or twice, nothing significant, except to him, and he flunked me and said, with a grin, I could retake the test again in six months. When I took the paperwork back in to get a six-month learners permit for ten dollars, they said I could ride anywhere except on major freeways, during daytime only, and without a passenger. Since I did not plan on doing any of these three restrictions, I ended up just going back and renewing the learners permit every six months. The ten dollars was worth not giving that guy the satisfaction of flunking me again.

The area was great for motorcycle riding and I rode three or four times a week along the back roads of Pickens and Dawson Counties. I saw my first black bear when he crossed a Dawson County back road in front of me, and I saw a lot of both counties that car drivers would not have seen when I ventured up dirt roads and trails. One problem I had was that after about two hours of riding, my eyes would dry up and become irritated, because of the Glaucoma. I was unaware of this problem while riding cross country back in the late 70's, because I would run out of gas after two hours and have to stop sometime before that to fill up. Another problem proved to be more serious and ended my motorcycle adventure. Once or twice, after riding some distance, I went into Atrial Fib and had to pull off the road until the dizziness and nausea subsided to the point I could ride again. I would still be in Atrial Fib riding back home, but to a lesser degree. I made the mistake of asking my new cardiologist what I could do when this occurred and he gave me an ultimatum. Get rid of the motorcycle or find a new cardiologist! By this time I had started a job and was riding the bike less, so after talking it over with Sandy I listed the motorcycle on EBAY.

I listed it on EBAY without a picture, because I did not know how to do it, and only received a few inquiries. After the listing ran out, I got a call from a man in Illinois who was very interested in the Indian Chief Replica aspect. I mailed him a picture, which I knew how to do, and he bought the bike for my asking price. I never could figure out how anyone could by car or boat or motorcycle on EBAY without ever seeing it in person and test driving it, but apparently lots of people did. He said he would hire a transport service to come down and pick up the motorcycle and I agreed to send him the title after I received his check. The transport service got lost and arrived about eleven p.m. five miles down the road at the grocery store parking lot, which meant I had to ride the bike down there at night with a learner's permit that prohibited me riding at night. I had never ridden the bike at night which further complicated things. I had visions of getting pulled over by the Sheriff's that patrolled just outside the gates, or running off the unlit roads and wrecking the motorcycle.

Neither event occurred and I made it down to the parking lot in one piece. The transport service turned out to be a very large pickup truck towing a long trailer that could hold three large cars. I rode the bike inside the empty trailer and the driver secured it to a special apparatus designed to hold a number of motorcycles. We got to talking and he said he was on his way to Florida to pick up some more motorcycles and a car, before returning back north. When I asked him if he could make much money transporting motorcycles, he said he had recently taken five very expensive bikes down to Daytona, Florida, for a man that planned to attend the big motorcycle rally held there every year, and charged him $1,000 per bike. When they got down there, the man looked around and, not liking what he saw, asked him how much he would charge to store the bikes in his trailer during the two day rally. Without giving it much thought, he told the man $5,000 because he really did not want to hang around down there, and the man said "done." The driver said he could have kicked himself for not saying $10,000, because the man would probably have paid that much.

The transport driver also told me he transports multiple motorcycles out to Sturgis, South Dakota, for the big annual motorcycle rally, where riders from all over North America come to party. He takes them to one of the small towns near Sturgis, where the riders roll around in the dirt and mount their bikes to ride the last few miles to the rally, alleging to have ridden from the east coast. He waits for them to return a few days later, and transports them back east, all for a hefty fee, of course. But the big money is in transporting pro athlete's cars from city to city when their team goes on the road. Some of the high paid athletes cannot stand to be without their showy expensive cars, he said. Having run out of stories, I bid the transporter farewell and called a sleepy Sandy to come get me, and thus concluded, I thought, the final chapter on my motorcycle story. I had come from flipping over the handle bars of the original Indian Chief my college roommate had given me, to riding the Honda 150 street bike cross country, to owning and selling an Indian Chief replica; over a 33 year span. However, the story did not end that night! A week later I received a call from my bike's new owner. He wanted to know if I knew anything about the scratches along the right side of the bike. I told him it was news to me and had a receipt from the transporter that stated the bike was intact without any visible damage. He surmised that perhaps something had happened at the storage facility where the bike was delivered, and that was that. So much for buying vehicles on EBAY!

For some time after the "motorcycle/swimming/golf phase of my Big Canoe life, I was content with walking Oliver two or three days a week, being Mr. Mom, working on the outdoor train layout and making Costco runs with my neighbor down the street. My association with the neighbor started at Mexican Train sessions during which we engaged in friendly banter back and forth. This escalated into trips to Costco, in faraway Cummings, a 45 minute drive. What started as lunch at Costco turned into lunch at a different place each time out. Uncle Al, as I called him, turned into a friendship that still exists with him in Texas and me in Georgia. After a visit to us in Soleil a few years back, he was so impressed with our immediate neighborhood and friendly neighbors that they moved into a Del Webb over 55 community. They had originally moved from Big Canoe to a well-rounded community in Texas because they wanted to be around stimulating younger people who would keep them young. What they found were mostly techy foreigners who left for work every morning and kept to themselves on weekends.

ANOTHER NEW CAREER

One of the perks Sandy received for being in upper management at Big Canoe was use of the amenities free of charge, for both her and her spouse. On top of the lot and house assessments, the amenities of golf, tennis, fitness center, swim and beach club, etc., were ala carte and quite pricey. I took advantage of the golf and swimming amenities from day one, but soon felt guilty about Sandy working full time while I played all day. I had assumed house cleaning and laundry duties, and was soon cooking four nights a week, but was not contributing financially except for my newly acquired Social Security monthly check. It must be a man-thing, but it irked me not to "pay my own way," so to speak. I looked into doing some health care administration consulting for the small hospitals in the area, but having been out of the action for eight years and small hospitals aversion to big city consultants killed that idea.

The Pickens County Developmental Officer lived in Big Canoe and sought out Sandy and I to come over "for a glass of wine" (a very common invitation in BC we soon found out) one night. He had found out about our Country Inn experience and thought we ought to pursue buying and operating a large historical estate, The Tate House, located in Pickens County, about 20 minutes from BC. The furnished estate sat unused, except for an occasional special event, and was just begging to be reactivated as a Bed and Breakfast and restaurant. A wealthy family had purchased the then vacant estate for their daughter to renovate and turn into a flourishing business. The only problem was that the daughter had no intention of working 24/7, and wanted no part of their "gift". We did take a tour of the estate and it was unique, with a lot of potential. The main house was constructed out of pink marble from the nearby marble mines, but the estate overall still required a lot of renovation and a huge marketing effort. We did give it some thought, about thirty seconds worth, and decided we had been there and done that.

One night Sandy came home and mentioned that the golf pro was looking for an older man to work in the golf operation as a "cart boy." This was a position that brought up, and returned, golf carts from the cart barn, and paid $7.50 an hour and free golf. I was getting free greens fees because of Sandy, but had to pay $16.00 for the cart. With this job I would get the cart free also. It would also make me a wage earner again; not the major wage earner, but a contributor, at least. Once I got rid of the motorcycle, I needed something else to do, so I took the job. I would not work weekends, when Sandy was at home, but that was all right because they had enough kids on weekends during the school year. The cart barn was a low shed built into the side of a hill facing Lake Petite and parallel to the clubhouse, which housed the small pro shop and cart storage area. Most of the golf carts were parked outside in a small parking area just below the cart barn adjoining a maintenance building where the carts were serviced and repaired.

I reported to work around eight in the morning and joined a man even older than me, who had come in at the crack of dawn to open up and have some carts ready for the early bird golfers. If a tournament was scheduled, he would come in even earlier to set up enough carts for a shotgun start. Billy was his name and bullshit was his game. Billy had helped build most of the roads in Big Canoe during the late sixties and early seventies and was a fixture among the long term residents. In addition to his golf job, he pet sat for a lot of the longtime residents, so just about everybody knew "old Billy." As such, he had the dirt on any resident or Big Canoe employee that had dirt to uncover. Billy loved to talk, so pretty soon I knew more about things I should not have been privy to. I knew the golf pro and his assistant were ripping off the Property Owners Association (which was me, by the way) by selling golf balls and clubs, under the table, to residents and others, and that the golf pro was running a Ponzi scheme locally for a man in Florida. I knew who was screwing whose wife, including the golf pro, and who cheated at cards. Billy was a cornucopia of information, some of which was even true, and some of it was about himself.

He professed to having hauled moonshine on the back roads of Dawson and Pickens Counties as a teenager, during the waning days of mountain stills and bootlegging. There was actually an old still located on one of the seven mountains in Big Canoe. Some of the other drivers were supposedly the initial NASCAR drivers, according to the NASCAR museum in Dawsonville, and Billy. He had an Asian girlfriend, younger than himself and better off financially, who once bought him a big hot tub for his trailer, but he did not want it. He left it outside and filled it with dirt to grow tomatoes in. Billy was the local authority on growing tomatoes in the awful red clay soil that pervaded the two counties.

One of the "cart boys" that came on duty after school let out and on weekends was actually a pretty sixteen year old girl who was "servicing" the assistant golf pro. The Assistant Pro insisted she wear tight cut-off jeans and a tank top that left very little to the imagination. They would go down to the maintenance shed together, on some pretense, and the door would get locked for a brief period. He would come out smiling and she would just cum out. The assistant Pro was married with a child and one in the oven, and he eventually left his wife after the second child was born, and allegedly married the teenager. Things did not change much in the rural environments, and Mercersburg came to mind with its teenage girl pregnancy problem.

The teenaged girl was rewarded for her loyalty by getting to drive the machine that scooped up the balls off the driving range and to run the ball washing machine, which just happened to be behind the maintenance shed. She was not allowed to ride the machine up the hillside at the back end of the driving range to retrieve balls. That chore was reserved for the more adventurous, and expendable, male contingent. She was also not subject to the usual target practice by those hitting balls off the driving range tees. To make sure, her first pass would always be closest to the tee boxes, and she would wave so they knew it was a young girl driving the machine. The rest of us were subjected to a constant barrage of balls directed at us by resident golfers hoping to crack a windshield or nail the driver when he stopped to clear a clogged scoop. I knew this from having been on both the receiving end and the delivery end, when I would be cleaning or using the driving range.

At this point in time, Big Canoe was using gas golf carts and part of my job was to gas up the carts at the end of the day, or some sooner if they were not going to be used again that day. There was a 500-gallon gas tank located on the far side of the maintenance shed, not more than ten yards from the lake. Any gas spills, of which there were many, trickled directly into Lake Sconti. That lake emptied into a stream that filled a retention pond that eventually fed a water treatment plant for Big Canoe. The stream also continued on to merge with other streams to empty into the Chattahoochee River. Most all of the waterways and lakes in Georgia, and in big canoe, are controlled by the Corps of Engineers, who frowned on any kind of contamination of their precious waterways. In addition to spillage of gasoline into the lake, some gas was spilling into the gas tanks of cars belonging to the Golf Pro and his Assistant. I am sure spillage was not the main reason that the POA Board switched to battery operated carts. Battery operated carts were supposedly more efficient….on eighteen holes of a hill course? It took several various combinations of batteries before a cart would dependently make it around eighteen holes of that hillside golf course.

My cart boy job only lasted three or four months, until about the end of October when the days got shorter and the temperature began to cool down, and older golfers began to hibernate for the winter. The golf Pro approached me with an offer to supervise the dwindling cart boy crew because they were becoming difficult to manage without onsite oversite. It was a title only, without an increase in pay or golf privileges, so I took the opportunity to bail. I had started up another venture by then, and was doing some minor marketing along with a neighbor. My neighbor, two houses up the street, was running a one-man house inspection business, and said there was a real need in Big Canoe for a house sitting business. There were many residents who split their time between Big Canoe and Florida, and their homes sat empty for up to six months at both ends.

I had to incorporate again in Georgia under Grantz-Filkowski Property Management, Inc., to get a business license for the new entity, House Sitters, Inc. My neighbor, Nelson, would take me to the Jasper Chamber of Commerce meetings and introduce me around, but I never officially joined. I posted flyers around Big Canoe, but did not get the response I expected, in spite of offering a low ball price. One day I got a call from a man who lived in Holland and had just purchased a small cabin high up on one of the mountains in Big Canoe. He and his family would only use the cabin two or three weeks a year and they were looking for someone to keep an eye on the place. We agreed on two visits a month during which I would run the water, flush the toilets, do a walk-through looking for pests, mold, broken windows, etc. Soon after, I got a call from an attorney in Florida who had just purchased a new five bedroom house in the newest section of BC. He filled it with new expensive furniture, flat panel T.V's in every bedroom, and an expensive sound system throughout the house. He planned to rent the house out to guests coming to BC for weddings, family gatherings, bachelor parties, or whatever. I cautioned him against this idea as we had just had a house in BC burned down by a group of sorority sisters who had rented it for a reunion weekend. They built a huge fire in the fireplace, after a night of drinking and smoking pot that got out of control and spilled over onto the roof. There were also other instances of groups trashing the rented houses during their "event," and creating disturbances, for which the property owner was responsible and liable for.

The attorney said that was what insurance was for, and he was looking for someone that would also clean up the place after the guests had left. I told him that was not my thing and he needed to contact a rental agency who did this as part of their contract. He replied that these agencies charged too much and he wanted to rent the place himself to protect his investment; which did not make much sense to me. I could see the handwriting on the wall with my new venture, and did not actively seek additional business, thereafter. Interestingly though, two other BC residents started up a similar business within a month of my flyers appearing. Driving up that mountain twice a month to serve my only client proved to be a pain, especially in the winter, but I stuck with it and eventually Sandy and I became good friends with the Hollanders.

Not too much later, another opportunity came up when the husband of the gal that managed the Marina came down with terminal cancer and she had to take a leave of absence to take care of him. He had helped her with some of the physical aspects of the job, as they were BC residents that lived just up the hill from the Marina, and he was close enough to come down and help when summoned. It was not a full time position and done more on an as-needed basis, so I agreed to $1000 per month for a six month period.

The Marina was a 110 slip old wooden structure located in a cove just south of the dam on Lake Petit. Residents could rent the boat slips dirt cheap and most did so because it was cheaper than storing their boat somewhere, even at the POA storage facility. The POA also had a rental fleet that consisted of five large pontoon boats, some canoes, and some flat bottomed Jon Boats that people took out for fishing. The developer also kept a large pontoon boat at the Marina that he allowed the POA to rent out if his company was not using it. The Jon Boats and the pontoon boats were powered by small battery powered electric motors: one to a Jon Boat and two to a pontoon boat. There was also a smaller Marina at the opposite end of the lake that held 120 canoe racks for residents to rent to store their own canoes, and a single old wooden dock. At this time there was not a shed or storage facility on either site to purchase bait, ice, or goodies. All boat rentals were handled by the fitness center, but slip and canoe rack rentals were handled by the "Marina Meister", which was now me.

In addition to the above, I would do a walk- through of both marinas in the morning to look for boats sinking, becoming loose from their mooring, missing, or canoes blown off their racks. I would check in at the fitness center and check on rentals so that I was present when they left, and came back in to the marina. I was responsible for cleaning up the rental after they came in, if the renter did not do so, as instructed. I also had to be available to go out in the lake to rescue stranded rental and guest boats using a gasoline powered Jon Boat. Fortunately, there was not any swimming allowed in either this lake or Lake Sconti, so I did not have to be a lifeguard. As in other aspects of my life experiences, I could write a book on my career as Marina Meister at Big Canoe.

Fishing was a big thing on all three lakes, but really big on Lake Petit where the Marinas were, because this lake was stocked twice a year with brown trout. There was not any fishing allowed on the boat slips or the boats berthed in the slips because of fishing lines either loose and floating around, or attached to fishing poles, getting tangled in the electric motors. Fish parts and bait lying around on the berth decks just added another potential hazard to the already hazardous old wooden walkways. You had to purchase an annual fishing pass from the POA and also have a valid state fishing license to fish on the lakes. Fishing was actually an amenity along with golf, tennis, fitness, swimming, etc. There was a limit of four fish per person per day, although I guess you could take home your first limit and return for more.

Fishing and boating were monitored by Public Safety, of which I was an extension of, and reported to. There was also Marshall Dillon, a volunteer who took it upon himself to safeguard the interests of the POA from poachers and limit violators. He was a twenty-year retired Navy Shore Patrol veteran who never quite got it out of his system. He carried a sidearm that was not sanctioned, but anyone in Georgia can carry a visible sidearm, and disliked renters and guests that dared to fish in "his lakes." He was also a personal friend of the couple that ran the Marina and was determined that I do things their way, which of course, I did not. I kind of kept him out of the main marina, but I could not keep him from challenging fishermen along the lake banks and dam, and over at the other small marina. He would demand to see a fisherman's fishing pass and license and look for limit violations or people swimming off the boats. Nobody seemed to challenge him because he was dressed in a uniform he designed and carried that gun. The POA tolerated the many complaints they received about his negative approach to people because he was a volunteer, I guessed. He did get to berth his pontoon boat at the marina free of charge, however, so he was not strictly a volunteer.

I completed my six months plus another month or two because the husband took longer to die than anticipated. The winter months were a trial when temperatures dropped into the teens and the wind howled across the lake. Ice would form on the decking and in, or on, the boats and make walking difficult. Boat rentals stopped during the winter but slip renewal time and paperwork made up for that. The following summer I did another brief stint at the marina when the woman decided to pack it in and the POA was doing a search for her replacement. The marina operation was not a priority of the POA at that time and they were not willing to commit funds or manpower to improve things. I had submitted several suggestions on ways to improve service and increase revenues, but all had been ignored. The only suggestion they followed up on was when I offered to assist in the operation of the outdoor storage facility as part of my duties as Marina Meister. The storage facility was mismanaged and in poor physical condition because the volunteer running it was a long term volunteer they did not want to upset, and have to hire someone to replace him. I immediately made enough changes to antagonize him into leaving, and the job was merged into the Marinameister job description.

The storage facility contained boats, RV's, cars, trucks and pickups, and some building materials and landscape materials from contractors that were not allowed to be there. The inventory list of who was supposed to be where and paying what was a mess, and in straightening it out I discovered a fairly new red pickup truck not on the books. While attempting to straighten out the paperwork, the red pickup truck was broken into and the stereo equipment stolen. Residents were paying for a secured storage facility that was not very secure, apparently. I finally located the owner of the red pickup and it turned out to be the golf pro at our golf complex. He said he was storing the truck at our facility because he was planning on giving it to his daughter, and that the truck had been given to him by a friend in Florida. When I told him it had been broken into and I was going to report the theft to the Sheriff's office, he told me not to do that. A red flag went up at that point and I called it in anyway.

A deputy came out and did his thing and found out the truck had been reported stolen. That was the beginning of the end for the golf pro. Among other things, he was found to be running a Ponzi scheme locally for a Florida man, and had taken some Big Canoe residents and some employees for large sums of money. The golf pro ended up wearing an orange jump suit in a Florida jail.

It was about this time we experienced a severe thunderstorm and the roof of the clubhouse took a lightning strike above the golf office. A fire started immediately in the attic space, and eventually spread quickly and burned the 1970's structure to the ground. The Property Owner Association had already been talking about replacing the antiquated clubhouse before the fire, and when the insurance company found this out, they began to make noise about arson. Fortunately, someone knew that the National Weather Service records every lightning strike in the country, and when petitioned, reported that the clubhouse had been hit by two lightning strikes, back-to-back. End of discussion!

The resulting rebuilding of the clubhouse was a disaster due mostly to an overabundance of input by property owners. Design and construction by committee just does not work, and Big Canoe had to learn this by experience.

The only good thing that came out of the process was Sandy's reputation as a shrewd negotiator and astute business person. This became known at an annual meeting of Property Owners, when the Board Chairman reported that the insurance company had finally settled for the clubhouse fire, but only if the Board promised that Sandy would stop coming back with new demands to increase the settlement figure. She had managed to raise their original one million dollar figure to $4.5

million over the year since the fire.

The restaurant function of the clubhouse was transferred over to the swim club, which had a small kitchen capable of putting out a limited menu. Sandy was given responsibility for this operation, because of our Inn experience, in addition to her financial duties. As many of the POA employees worked in food and beverage and the swim club, Sandy eventually also became head of a new Human Relations, or Personnel, function at the POA. Again, in addition to her financial duties!

Out of boredom or frustration, or an opportunity to see more of my wife, I volunteered for a couple of committees and was in the second "Leadership Big Canoe" class. "Leadership Big Canoe" was an attempt at educating property owners about Big Canoe and the Property Owners Association, to prepare them for volunteer roles on various committees and task forces. I sat on the "Long Range Planning Committee", "Assisted Living" Task Force, and "Waste Management" Task Force that came up with a very successful innovative single stream recycling program that saved the POA a lot of money.

Sandy also found time to volunteer her services at the Big Canoe Chapel and was Treasurer for the Women's Guild big annual fund raiser that raised over $100,000 that year. This money went to scholarships for every graduating senior in the Pickens and Dawson County school systems. She eventually trained for and became a Steven's Minister in the Chapel's program, and was mentoring a depressed older lady when we left Big Canoe.

If all this was not enough, she began teaching Accounting at night at a new Catholic college that had started up in nearby Dawson County. She had always wanted to be a college professor and this was an opportunity she could not pass up. All of this was reminiscent of our time in Danville when she worked full-time while pregnant with Megan, had three teenagers at home, and pursued her MBA at night and Saturdays. She still gets upset when I call her a "type A" personality.

Growing Old in America

NOT ALL WORK AND NO PLAY

Believe it, or not, we actually found time to socialize and get away for vacations. We drove up to New York to attend my oldest sister's 50th Wedding Anniversary shortly after my TURP procedure in 2004, while I was still wearing a catheter and bag. Needless to say, there was no dancing by me at the Polish Community Center function. We had a nice post-function get together with my two sisters and bother, and it proved to be the last time the four siblings got together. I later attended my 47 ½ year High School reunion down in Marco Island, Florida, shortly after arriving back in Big Canoe from the big apple, but without the catheter and bag. The lowlight of that trip was encountering my high school sweetheart for the first time in 47 ½ years and her remarking "but, you look so old." I returned the favor 2 ½ years later at the 50th reunion (we were having reunions every 2 ½ years because of the high attrition rate) when she sat next to me at dinner and across from another former beau. When she commented that she did not recognize any of the other men in the room, I replied that I had found that difficult to believe since she had dated all of them before leaving high school. I may have used another word in place of "dated", but am not sure.

Sandy started out 2005 by driving back to California with her father, who had come east to visit us and the lady he had met at the Inn a year earlier. He had been calling this woman long distance on his cell phone almost daily and running up huge phone bills. Sandy spent only a few days out there helping him clean out her mother's things, which had gone untouched since her death in 1997, and to prepare his condo for selling it. The plan was to sell the condo and move her father back to either live with us or move into a Life Care Center an hour east of Big Canoe. Later that summer, I flew back to California to help Sandy's dad sell his condo and drive back with some of his furniture in his van. The condo sold in two days, thanks to me talking his neighbor into buying it, and her father moved in with a woman he had met in a grocery store.

I drove back in his loaded Dodge Caravan pulling a trailer with a freezer, washer, dryer, china closet, and small items of furniture. I had already made this trip several times in my life and would be making it many more. The next opportunity to travel highway 40 westward came a few months later when I drove back to California in the Dodge to pick up Sandy's father and some more of his personal items. He had decided to move into the Life Care Center near us, but neglected to share his hidden agenda with Sandy or myself, or the previous roommate he had just left.

Upon arrival, he was interviewed, financial analyzed, and accepted at Lanier Village, after plunking down a $95,000 deposit. It would take about a week to repaint and make some minor renovations to his apartment at the Life Care Center, and the plan was to spend that time living with us. With Sandy at work, he awoke the next morning and initiated his hidden agenda by calling his east coast girlfriend to announce his arrival in Georgia and find out when she would be moving down to join him at Lanier Village. Apparently, she informed him she had no intention of doing so, and hung up. He then announced to me that he would be returning to California to marry the grocery store woman he had been living with. I informed him that I was not about to drive him back to California, and at age 83 he jumped into his Dodge Caravan and took off for the West Coast. Sandy had to do some fast talking to get her father's $95,000 deposit back.

Sandy and I celebrated our 25th wedding anniversary, in June of 2006, aboard the brand new Queen Mary II on a Mediterranean cruise. We knew the ship had a huge ball room and took ball room dancing lessons before the cruise. The first time we went down to the ball room, we were shocked to find the dance floor full of really good dancers, almost professional. Needless to say, we did not do much ball room dancing on that trip.

Later on that year, we drove up to the Denver area to celebrate Thanksgiving at my niece's home. My sister Eileen and her husband flew out from New York, and my brother, who lives in the Denver area, were present for dinner and we had a mini family reunion. In Colorado, everyone seems to have at least two large dogs and they accompany you everywhere. At any given time, we had a mixture of seven labs and golden retrievers in the house, along with our Chihuahua Oliver. Despite his size, Oliver ruled the roost and one bark from him sent the others scrambling for cover.

We made several trips up North over the next few years to visit my sisters, as their health declined. On one of these trips, we revisited Mercersburg and drove around the Inn parking lot without going inside. We had heard the new owners changed a lot of things, including removing the almost 100 year old boxwood hedge that circled the herb garden at the rear entrance, and decided we wanted to remember the place as we left it.

In 2008 Sandy turned 60 and I threw her a surprise dinner party for 40 people at the new clubhouse. She was totally surprised, and mortified, after complaining to me frequently that I had never done anything for her "big O" occasions, while she had parties for me on my 40th, 50th, and 60th birthdays. Her biggest surprise, however, came when we got the bill for the clubhouse party.

Earlier that year, we rented a house in Myrtle Beach that was actually on the beach. I had specified to the rental agency that it had to be situated such that you walked out the door right onto the beach. Dana and the five year old twins were coming and I wanted them to have that experience. The rental house was indeed on the beach, but with a fifteen story condo building on each side of it. Apparently, most ocean front property in resort areas eventually turns into multi-story condos.

In March of 2009, we went to Costa Rica with three other couples from our street. Sandy and I had bid on this trip at a fund raising dinner the year before after consuming too much wine, and tried to soften the economic hit by inviting our neighbors to buy in. We had a fabulous experience in spite of never having traveled with any of these people beforehand. Highlights of the trip to the mountain retreat included paying more for mandated car insurance than the rental fee on the rented car, being limited to 25 pounds of luggage (plus there was a limit on your combined weight and luggage) on the small plane that carried us to the closest airstrip to the destination, travel by car at 25 miles per hour for hours on a rock graveled road, frogs in the toilets and geckos on the walls, and running out of water due to power failures. Enough alcohol was consumed, however, to make all these minor inconveniences acceptable. Sandy figured out how all four couples could write off their portion as a charitable contribution, and everyone was happy. Later on we discovered that we could have taken that trip for a fraction of what we bid.

That summer, we made our annual trek to California where we would celebrate my 70th birthday. We drove out that year in a Dodge Caravan that we purchased from Lauri and Kevin when they bought a new van. Sandy, the sneaky one, arranged to celebrate my 70th (once again she outshone me) at a resort up close to Yosemite on this trip. One of my college roommates and his wife came up to our cabin spur of the moment when Dana and the twins were already there, and somehow we all travelled to this resort for a drink. Sandy had arranged to have my other two roommates and their wives at the resort and the celebration began. After the dinner and wine and countless stories, Dana suggested to me that I write down these stories for the rest of the family and friends to enjoy, and thus began the writing of these three books.

The other major event to happen that summer occurred a week after the 70th celebration, when Sandy's ex-husband, Al, and his wife came up to our cabin for a visit. It seemed that Sandy felt that we needed another pair of hands to perform maintenance on the cabin since her brother in Cambria had no inclination to do so and I had hit the big 7-0! The end result was Al agreeing to open up the cabin in the summer and close it in the fall, in exchange for using the place when we were not present. This provided fuel for my allegations that Sandy was going to remarry her ex-husband when I kicked the bucket.

Smaller trips to Destin Florida, Savanna Georgia and a trip up to Chattanooga Tennessee for Sandy to go parasailing, at age 61, ended travel for a while. Sandy was towed up to 3000 feet by an ultralight and parasailed down with her instructor to the valley floor to close out 2009. The following year would include a big trip for the family, but without me.

The big trip came in May of 2010 when Sandy went to Greece with a group from the Big Canoe Chapel to follow the Apostle Paul's travels through that region. Because I elected not to go along (too many foreigners over there), I suggested she take daughters Lauri and Megan with her. I did not think either one would go on a trip with a bunch of old religious types, but it would have been a nice gesture. Both accepted the free trip with Mom, however, and the old bank account took a big hit. Sandy then decided that the third daughter, Dana, who could not go because she was prosecuting a case, should not be left out and sent her a check for the trip amount. This was during the economic downturn and that made matters even worse. It would have saved us some money if I had just agreed to go. Sandy estimated we lost around $250,000 during that seven year period, 2006 – 2013, from our stock market investments.

The three of them shared a room and a cabin on the boat portion of the trip, and I took bets on which one would crack first. They all had a great time and were even talking to each other at the end of the trip. The mostly senior tour loved the two girls and they, in turn, enjoyed the seniors. Apparently, the common denominator was wine which made me rethink my decision not to go. Sandy said it was the best trip she had ever taken!

In late July and August of that year, we piled in the old van and drove out for our annual trip to California, but this time we wound through Texas, Arizona, and Southern California looking at ten over 55 communities. Sandy had a desire to move back to California, at some point, to be closer to her father and brother. This was not to be in the immediate future, but we became experts on the Del Webb and Trilogy communities. During that trip we experience the phenomena that the further west we drove the more expensive it got to keep a pet in your motel/hotel room. In Texas it was $25, then $50 in Arizona, and finally $100 at a Marriot in California. That has since changed as the industry finally realized that a lot of people travel with pets, and the access has increased with prices coming down.

Upon returning to Georgia that year, it became apparent the old van would not survive another trip to California and I purchased a 2006 Chevrolet Suburban for future road trips, thus keeping alive our propensity to purchase low-mileage "previously owned" vehicles. I bought this car from a guy I played poker with and it came with four months remaining on Sirius Radio. I could now drive around listening to 50's and 60's music and reminisce about growing up. The Suburban came in handy during 2011 when the first road trip was to drive Megan up to New Hampshire in March to scout the Dartmouth campus and places for her to live. Megan had accepted a job at Dartmouth, with a big raise in salary and a signing bonus, to head up a new research project. A few months later we all traveled up there to move her into her new apartment. We originally were going to tow her car up on a flatbed trailer, but were unable to load it on the trailer because the car was customized and too low to the ground. It proved to be the "trip to hell" with four of us crammed into the Suburban with Oliver and Megan's dog and cat (both uncrated), and all of Megan's belongings that were supposed to be in the trailered car. Megan's long-term boyfriend elected not to accompany her to New Hampshire and the apparent termination of that relationship put a cloud on the trip up.

On the first trip up to New Hampshire we stopped to visit my oldest sister in Pennsylvania in the nursing home, and on the way back from the second trip we stopped to see my sister with the brain tumor. After these two visits I had seen the future and was not looking forward to it.

That spring of 2011 we flew out to Palm Springs and looked at over-55 housing, and spent a week checking out that entire area. While there, we ran into a woman on the street with a long haired Chihuahua puppy that she wanted to give away. Sandy fell in love with it and it took some talking on my part to talk her out of a plane ride, with a stopover in Denver, with a puppy. That summer our California road trip included a trip to Paso Robles to check out housing, and it became our new future destination. I actually joined a wine club at a local winery out there in anticipation of a move to that area. There was a narrow window of opportunity when house prices remained low enough for us to consider the area. Upon our return to Georgia, I drove up to Connecticut for my 55th high school reunion. The numbers attending were dwindling and the stories were becoming harder to remember, but for a few days we were all seventeen again. To illustrate how frail we had all become, while at the big dinner I sat next to a female classmate and teased her about her having taught me how to French kiss. Two weeks later she died in a hospital from pneumonia.

Travel in 2012 followed the same pattern as the two previous years almost. In March we traveled down to the Sarasota/Fort Meyers area of Florida to check out more over-55 communities, and also spent some time on the Sanibel Island gulf coast area. We came home to Georgia and added Florida to our growing list of places to relocate to. In July we took a fifteen day riverboat cruise on the Rhine River throughout Europe, highlighted by free beer and wine, to my delight. A week after returning we took off in the Suburban for California and the cabin.

In October, I flew out to San Francisco to attend a memorial service/party for a college friend and teammate who passed away from the brain tumor I had helped diagnosis some 35 years previously. He had specified a party at the Irish-American Club in San Francisco upon his death, for the players he had coached and the teammates he had played with. It was one hell of a party for one hell of a guy. This was the third of my football teammates to pass on. Later that month, Sandy and I flew up to Denver to attend my niece's wedding, a first time marriage for both of them in their forties. Both my older brother and middle sister were there, with my older Sister attending via skype. The last time we all communicated together, but not in person this time. The Denver "wedding trip" ended our travel for a while due to a lot of reasons, some good and some not so good.

Growing Old in America

"DEATH TAKES A HOLIDAY" BUT NOT IN BIG CANOE

As stated earlier, I was able to join various social groups such as golf and poker as a replacement due to someone dying or becoming seriously ill. With the average age of Big Canoe residents being 63 this was not to be unexpected, but it was not personal to me as I had not known these people. During the following nine years here, however, our personal involvement with death increased considerable. We both aged ten years, putting me in the 74 age bracket, so this was not that unusual. This trend would continue going forward, naturally, but during the initial ten year period death certainly got my attention. Sandy's mom had died in 1997, while we were still at the Inn. Somewhat prematurely at the age of 75, but still considered to be "elderly." Now we found ourselves in a "senior" community attending memorial services for people we knew on a regular basis.

From 2004 to 2013 while in Big Canoe, three close football teammates and one of my college roommates passed on. My old roommate was severely overweight and a functioning alcoholic who elected to live his life the way he wanted to. He was told to lose 100 pounds because he could not fit on the Cath lab table and he refused to do it. Unable to determine the extent of his cardiac distress, he died at an age three years younger than mine. Six or seven of my surviving high school classmates died and numerous Big Canoe acquaintances met their maker. Sandy's dad passed on a month after we moved out of Big Canoe, followed closely by my brother-in-law; and my middle sister, within the next six months. About a year later my oldest sister died, and that left my older brother and me as the surviving members of our immediate family. My brother died two years later and that left me as the sole survivor of our family. Death had become an "old friend" and viewed as the way things are. There is a quote somewhere that says "Death is life's greatest invention; it perpetually replaces the old with the new." Sandy's mom died on the day that her great grandson was born. I view death as inevitable and as I write this approaching 78, a matter of not if, but when.

Walt Filkowski

THE FINAL MOVE

2012 proved to be a year for the movers and shakers. We put our house on the market at the end of 2011 with a plan to move back to California. This decision was arrived at after bids came in for remodeling the kitchen at $100,000 plus, when we only paid $389,000 for the house. Sandy announced, for the third year in a row, that she was going to retire the following year. This was after she completed a course of study that made her a Stephen Minister in the Chapel. I announced I would not cut my hair until Sandy retired. Megan got bored and lonely with her job at Dartmouth and returned to Atlanta for another research job at Emory University, and to her old boyfriend. She completed her Master Degree in Forensic Psychology and applied nation-wide for a PhD program, which she planned to finance with the money we would give her in lieu of a big wedding. Her other two sisters chose big weddings ($25,000) instead of the money. Megan got married in a plain civil ceremony at the court house in downtown Atlanta, probably the only white couple to do so that day, and applied the money we gave her to pay off student loans." I will never leave Peachtree City until the boys graduate from high school" Lauri, announced at Thanksgiving that she and her family were moving to Australia on December 28th, where her husband had taken a job and left IBM.

I gave up on my "work in progress" outdoor railroad and finished my second book, <u>MAKING IT IN AMERICA.</u> As I was now an authority on the subject matter of my third book at age 72, I started on "<u>GROWING OLD IN AMERICA.</u> We began 2013 by cleaning out, and getting ready to sell, Lauri's Peachtree City four bedroom home. They practically gave away or threw away all their furniture and household items in their haste to get to Australia on schedule, in spite of our offer to help out. They sold back to the dealer their recently purchased top-of-the-line BMW at a huge loss even after we offered to sell it for them. We were not asked to be involved in the sale of their house; they did it long distance from Australia. The explanation of this behavior did not come until some months later.

At the suggestion of a friend, we checked out an over-55 community in nearby Canton. Soleil was a 300 home community taken over by a new developer after the original developer, Leavitt, went bankrupt during the seven year downturn in the early nineties. We liked the community and looked at several resale homes with an agent, one of which we really liked. When we called back about the house, it had sold and that ended our interest in Soleil

Without any improvement in the real estate market in sight, we planned to take our house in Big Canoe off the market when the current listing was up in April. Several days before the listing was to expire, we received an offer, and sold the house, after some negotiation, for what we paid for it, with a closing in mid-July. Sandy estimated we lost about $55,000 of improvements with the sale. With the house sold, Sandy decided to retire and that allowed her and me to fly out to California and buy a house. We started out looking in our first choice, Paso Robles, but that narrow window of financial viability had closed, as housing prices rebounded faster than in Georgia. It was the same in nearby Cambria, on the coast, where Sandy's brother lived. We returned to the Palm Springs area and found more reasonable pricing, particularly in the over-55 communities. We finally settled on a new home to be built in the Del Webb Community of Shadow Hills, in Indio, with a completion date scheduled for November of 2013. The plan was to store our furniture and live up at our cabin near Yosemite until the house was ready.

June involved a lot of packing, retirement and going away parties, and a trip up to the New York area to visit my sisters, possibly for the last time. In one of those "what were we thinking moments," we decided, once again, to rent a truck and move ourselves back to California, just as we had done when we moved some of our furniture from Santa Rosa to the Inn and from the Inn to Big Canoe. I would drive the truck and tow a car, and Sandy would follow in the packed suburban. Of course we were eighteen years younger and a little healthier back in 1996. The intent was to save on expense, as we had paid more for the new house in California than we had intended. To save even more moving expense we decided to hire some of the Big Canoe staff to load the truck and, as happened in Mercersburg, this proved almost fatal. We sold off a lot of our furniture, as we were going from a four bedroom 3600 square foot house to a two bedroom 2700 square foot dwelling. This was the first time we were actually downsizing to a smaller house, excluding the Inn. We were leaving behind the washer/dryer, refrigerator, garage freezer, and some outdoor furniture. Even so, the rented 28 foot Penske truck, that advertised holding the contents of a four bedroom house, proved woefully inadequate for what we had remaining to move.

What happened next turned out to be a "perfect storm" situation for disaster. During the final email negotiations on the sale of the Big Canoe house, the buyer changed the closing date to "the day of closing" which our realtor did not catch. That meant we had to be out the day of closing because the buyer's moving van was arriving the next day from New York. There already was some doubt that closing would occur because the buyers loan papers got fouled up somehow.

Then, a week before closing Lauri called from Australia and asked to be picked up at the airport on July 4th with her two teenaged sons. She planned to spend some time with us until she could rent a house back in Peachtree City and enroll the boys back in the high school they had left seven months earlier. It turned out her husband was an alcoholic and she left him because he would not stop drinking. Apparently, he was drunk during most of the moving process to Australia, which explained their erratic behavior during the move. Having sold off a lot of our furniture, including beds, we had to run out and buy two mattresses for the boys to sleep on and unpack sheets and towels and linens. They all moved out before our truck showed up.

On the day of our big move, the truck was late arriving at the Jasper office, which made us late to start loading, which was a minor complication compared to the two men that never showed up to load the now late truck. The two that did show up were elderly and Sandy and I had to help carrying stuff out to the truck. It proved to be a Chinese fire drill as I had planned to be inside the truck supervising the loading so as to make sure everything fit tightly and did not move around. We learned from our Inn move this would be necessary. Needless to say, dusk came and we were nowhere near finished loading and it became apparent that what was left would not fit into the truck. Sandy took charge and arranged to rent some storage units across from the North gate, borrow a pickup truck and put some neighbors to work loading and transporting items to the storage units. I woofed down a hamburger and finished some white wine while forgetting to take my heart pills. The cardiologist later decided that the exertion of moving furniture, stress, and not taking the pills put me in severe atrial fibrillation and I ceased functioning. A neighbor walked me down to her house and put me to bed. We were too busy to even consider going to the Emergency Room. Sandy and a friend of hers worked almost all night cleaning the house after it was emptied. The next morning Sandy went to the closing and it did close. She stopped off at the bank and deposited the check on the way back. I finished cleaning out the garage while still in atrial fib, in preparation for the arrival of the new owner's moving van. It was a slow process as I was not feeling that great.

That afternoon we retired to the neighbor's house that had offered to let us stay until I was well enough to travel. We kept checking to see what time the new owner's moving van showed up, but the day passed without it arriving. The moving van did not arrive the next day, or the day after. We heard that the new owner was beside herself because no one knew where the truck was, including the moving company. The truck did not arrive until six weeks after the closing date! All our rushing around had been in vain. We never heard about what had happened to the moving van.

Our great plan to move ourselves across the country, transfer our belongings and furniture into a storage facility, and stay at our mountain cabin near Yosemite while our new house was being built in Indio, was no longer feasible. We had a second truckload of stuff in a storage unit across the street, my physical condition had deteriorated, and Sandy's daughter and two grandsons were back in Peachtree City with a marriage in doubt.

PLAN B

There was no way we could make it to California without considerable additional expense of a professional move and storage while the house in Indio was being completed, especially when construction had not even begun, we had recently found out. A completion date of late October was already pushing things, as snow would be falling by then and the cabin was inaccessible by middle November. Also, I would be of little use at a mountain cabin in my physical state.

We decided to ask our friends in Holland, whose cabin in Big Canoe we took care of in their absence, if we could stay in the cabin until we made a decision on what to do. Part of that decision making process included a trip over to Soleil to revisit the resale house we liked that had come back on the market after the sale had fallen through. Unfortunately, by the time we made it over to Soleil, the house had sold again. As long as we were there, we looked at the model homes and talked with an agent about the community. Before we knew it, the agent had us looking at available lots which could accommodate the model we liked. The model (Mansfield) we liked required some expensive upgrades which, the agent pointed out, would equal the price of a larger home that we really wanted but felt we could not afford. A new pod of lots was just opening up and several lots were still available, with three of them without a lot premium that also accommodated the larger home. The end result was we purchased a 2763 square foot ranch style house on a large corner lot for under $400,000, which put us under the threshold that seniors became except from paying school tax. Our annual property tax would be under $1000.

We were able to buy the Soleil house because Sandy had persuaded the Del Webb development in Indio, California, to let us out of our contract for the $450,000 house they were building for us. All they wanted was a letter from my cardiologist confirming that I had suffered a "heart attack". What I suffered was a "heart episode", which amounted to a severe atrial fib attack not requiring a visit to the emergency room (my insistence), or even a visit to the cardiologist (again, my decision). Obtaining a letter from my cardiologist seemed problematic; however, Del Webb screwed up and sent back our $50,000 deposit without ever receiving such a letter.

We negotiated a "utilities only" rental agreement with our Holland friends to stay in the Big Canoe cabin until April of 2014, and headed out to our own cabin in California to spend the summer. We did the usual raking an acre of pine straw from around the structures and trimming the pine trees up to four feet, but at a much more leisurely pace this time. With another California "no burn" in effect because of the fourth year of a draught, I had to get up early and complete burning in our burn pits before nine o'clock when the flyovers began and the lookout towers were manned. Burning was our only alternative as we could not dump on the State and National Park land surrounding us and were unable to trailer about 200 large garbage bags of debris down the mountain to the town dump. Most residents dumped in the Park land, but that was just transferring the problem outside our gates. Controlled burning was the better solution. We accomplished a lot of maintenance work on the cabin, in between visits from our eleven year old grandsons and visits to Yosemite and neighbors.

We planned on staying at the cabin until late October and be gone before the first snow arrived in early November. The weather turned wintery the last week in October and we packed up somewhat prematurely and planned to leave late the next morning after closing everything up for the winter. We woke up to a heavy snowfall with about two inches already on a frozen ground and the temperature in the teens. Closing down was speeded up considerably and we drove out the driveway in the suburban in 3-4 inches of unplowed snow that had fallen within an hour. The drive out the one mile of dirt road was perilous, but the two hour ride down the mountain was treacherous. The suburban did not have four wheel drive and It was the closest we had ever come to being snowed in or having an accident on the iced over, snow covered roads. The road trip back to Big Canoe was not without incident, as we received a phone call from our California daughter, Dana, who announced she had just been diagnosed with a brain tumor surrounding her optic nerve that was inoperable. The remainder of that trip back was spent worrying about Dana and the twins and facing the realization we were leaving one snowy mountain for another.

Walt Filkowski

SANDARLIN MOUNTAIN

The cabin belonging to our Holland friends was located some 3000 feet atop Sandarlin Mountain, one of the seven mountains in Big Canoe. Much of the winter the roads were iced over and it snowed frequently. At best it was under cloud cover most of the time and freezing or below; what were we thinking! A week after we arrived in November it snowed. The road up the mountain iced over, the steep side road down to the cabin driveway iced over, and the 45 degree driveway itself iced over. Needless to say, we spent a lot of time in that cabin until March of 2014. We watched a lot of T.V., built a lot fires, and I got to work a lot on Book III. Sandy knitted A LOT and cooked and baked a lot. Oliver suffered with quick trips out to go potty. We completed a bunch of jigsaw puzzles, played games on the computer and emailed everybody and anybody. Completion of the Soleil house was not anticipated until late March of 2014, some five months away. On days when it was not snowing, the wind not blowing, and the temperature above freezing, one of us would bundle up Oliver and take a walk around the hilly neighborhood. This meant walking up and down steep grades on narrow roads. Sandy was a walker, even then, and worked her way to walking up the main road to the top of the mountain, another two or three hundred feet of elevation.

Once or twice we found it necessary to get off the mountain for doctor's appointments and such, and I would have to shovel snow and ice off the 45 degree driveway. The main roads and side roads were usually plowed, or at the very least sanded. I would just shovel two lanes about eighteen inches in width to get up the driveway. Staying inside the lanes going up and coming down took some practice, and a few mishaps. I was still playing poker the first and third Tuesdays of the month in our ninth year of that game, subbing in another Cherokee neighborhood Monday night group, and playing Texas Hold-um on Thursday nights, at the clubhouse. Sandy and I also continued to play in our monthly Mexican Train group. All of this depended on being able to get up and down the mountain, of course.

The cabin itself was on the smallish size with a small master bedroom, bathroom, and kitchen/small living room/fireplace on the main floor. The basement had a large room with a fireplace, bathroom with a Jacuzzi tub, and storage closets. Above the kitchen area was a loft with sofa beds, TV, desk area, and walled-in storage under the roof line. There was a small deck area and a single-car carport. It was built in the early 1980's and showed its age. Part of the rental agreement included me performing maintenance as the need arose, and it arose from time-to-time. On one occasion, the hall ceiling light on the main floor quit working and it was not the bulb, switch, or the circuit breaker. When I went into the ceiling crawl space above the light, I found the wiring had shorted out and burned off the wire coating. The electrician I called in told us we were lucky the place had not burned down because someone had jury-rigged the wiring without a ground wire.

We managed to get off the mountain a few times, which corresponded to being able to get up the big hill leading into the Soleil development, to check on the progress on building our house. The hill was an 18% grade which we found out later was illegal and became an issue, along with some other road issues later on. We were fortunate to get one of the more competent building superintendents and he kept us up-to-date, even face booking us during the summer when we were at the California cabin. I made a visit one time, along with a Big Canoe neighbor, and found the cabinetry being installed in the kitchen and the cabinets on the floor in the laundry room, ready to be installed. The walls in the laundry room were marked for the cabinets, but at the wrong height. We had purchased a washer/dryer combination that sat on pedestals and required the cabinets to be higher than normal, a fact we had brought to the attention of our building superintendent some time earlier. I brought this to the installer's attention and he made the necessary height adjustment on the spot. This began a long list of construction problems that made us begin to question the ability of the construction superintendent to juggle the building of multiple houses at the same time, up to 17 to 20 at once.

Walt Filkowski

We closed out 2013 on top of that Damn Mountain, and put one of our more challenging years behind us. Sandy's dad had developed severe dementia, Papa Walt's heart problem, Lauri's family Australia adventure failure, and Dana's brain tumor did not make for a good year. A significant event occurred that year which escaped me at the time and did not become evident until years later. 2013 was the last year Tiger Woods won a professional golf event. I had become a Tiger fan during his glorious years and followed his game religiously. When Tiger's personal problems and injuries forced him out of golf, I lost interest in professional golf.

I had already lost interest in most sporting events, as they became less games and more and more entertainment. Television and the media in general, had taken over sports. The players began making enormous money and became prima donnas. The showboating and grandstanding after just about every play, was great for television, but not for me. The rules for professional basketball were changed to make the game more exciting and baseballs were altered to produce more homeruns. Professional football rules were changed to provide more offensive scoring because television ratings were going down. And then performance enhancing drugs entered the picture, and records books went out the window. To make matters worse, recreational drug usage seemed to go hand-in-hand with the growing salaries of athletes. With heightened media attention, sports came under the microscope and criminal activity, sexual and domestic abuse, and on and off the field activity, never before disclosed, became headlines. Unfortunately, this all trickled down to the college level and has tainted that arena, as well. While I loved sports growing up and well into my adult life, I cannot watch the entertainment version prevalent today.

Growing Old in America

WELCOME TO SOLEIL

February of 2014 finally arrived with the Soleil house set to close on the 14th, Valentine's Day. We had become concerned enough with the construction of our house, and several others in the neighborhood, to hire a building inspector to survey the house before the closing. I am not sure we got our money's worth as all he found wrong was a missing rafter in the roof. He lived in Soleil which was probably a mistake on our part, as we uncovered several defects in the walk-through with the construction superintendent and the Quality Assurance people. If ever there was an oxymoron that compared to the Central Intelligence Agency, it was the Developer's Quality Assurance program. When the quality people told us the missing rafter in the roof was taken out by the HAVAC crew to make room for some air ducts, we knew we were in trouble.

The walk-through was scheduled for the 13th, the day before closing, and had to be done before closing could occur. Closing was on a Friday and would have to be postponed until the following Monday because of the banks. The weather would dictate whether either event would occur. We had made arrangements for our kids and grandkids to help move us from the storage units over the weekend, the only time they were all available. Our mountain was iffy getting up the icy driveway in the cold morning, onto the steep icy side road, onto the icy main road down to the main gate. We called our building superintendent to find out if the 18% grade was doable with ice and snow, and he reported that he had made it up with some difficulty in his pickup truck earlier that morning, but that it should be o.k. with the sun out all morning.

We made it up the driveway and side road, down the main road to the gate, and on to Soleil without incident in the suburban. When we got to the steep grade, we wished we had four-wheel-drive because the sun had not done as good a job as we expected. Nevertheless, we made it up the two hills and on to 113 Mountain Laurel Court. The walk-through took two hours and revealed numerous cosmetic problems, which would take forever to resolve, as it turned out. The closing was verified for the next day and to be safe, we arranged to stay with friends down on Cherokee Drive in Big Canoe that night, in case the mountain froze over.

Closing was accomplished without incident and we met our kids and grandkids at the storage facility across from Big Canoe's north gate the next morning, with a U-Haul truck. We had three storage units at this site and had visited each one, on occasion, to locate an item or two. When items were stored on that fateful night of the "perfect storm", they were literally thrown in without any consideration for content or value.

On Saturday, February 14th, 2014, we officially moved into our house in the over-55 community of Soleil, located in Canton, Georgia, at my ripe old age of 74. We were the third completed house in the 32 house pod, and the first Trenton model on a slab. The only other Trenton model in Soleil was a basement version in another pod. As it turned out, twenty-two Trenton models were built in our pod, which soon became known as Trentonville in the Soleil Community. On our large corner lot we had two trees; the mandatory red maple and multi-trunk purple crepe myrtle, both planted by the developer, and duplicated on all 34 lots in the pod. We did not receive mail for the first few weeks at our new home because the house was originally platted to face the court that now bordered the right side of the house. However, that screw-up had a bright side as the developer ended up paying our community assessment that year because we did not exist.

We spent most of that spring and summer of 2014 out shopping for new furniture and rugs, and correcting the numerous construction foul-ups. Sandy planned all along to upgrade the kitchen appliances with Viking ovens, hood, and a free Viking dish washer that came with the package. We had purposely not added many upgrades during the building process, to keep the total cost of the house under the $400,000 threshold for being eligible for the county school tax exemption available to seniors. Our property tax for the first few years remained under $1000 as a result, and paid for many of the subsequent upgrades we made to the house. Another monetary source for the upgrades was the finder's fee the developer paid for bringing in buyers for their homes. We brought in six buyers from Big Canoe and earned seven thousand dollars in finder's fees. They reduced the fee after our fifth buyer and then all together shortly thereafter. After a visit to a home improvement show in Atlanta, we embarked on an extensive landscape and hardscape project that included extending out the rear patio and covering it with stamped concrete. A small waterfall, stone fireplace, and adjustable aluminum pergola completed the hardscape.

By this time I was about two years into growing a pony tail, the first item on my bucket list. After three years of Sandy telling me she was going to retire, In 2011 I told her I would cut my hair when she did so. I was a curiosity item when we moved into Soleil and became known as "the guy with the ponytail". I kept it growing until January of 2015 when I cut it off and donated the hair to a kid's medical wig program. My pony tail had grown down below my shoulder blades and, when not tied up in a tail, was quite a site. After the fact, I found out most of the hair donated for medical related wigs is either discarded or shipped overseas for other purposes. Years later, I am still sometimes referred to "as the guy with the ponytail".

During that first year in Soleil, we joined just about everything available in this "active adult community". God forbid we not live up to the expectations of being active. I joined a cooking club, started playing poker at the club house, and started playing golf again, while Sandy joined the garden club, exercised in the fitness center, and volunteer one day a week at Must Ministries, a homeless support center. Sandy also baked bread which she used to welcome each new resident to our 34-house pod, in which we were the third to be occupied. We both took up pickle ball and participated in just about every social event offered. We also kept in contact with Big Canoe with me continuing with the Tuesday morning poker game twice a month and Sandy doing her Steven's Ministry and blanket ministry at the Big Canoe Chapel. We also became more active in the nearby Reinhardt College music concerts because of its close proximity and our association with a faculty member.

I had promised Sandy when we left the Inn that I would attend religious services with her and pretty much did this the nine years we were in Big Canoe. Now it was time to find a local church and we shopped around for a Methodist Congregation a few Sundays. We chose a small church on the Reinhardt College campus over a much larger church with all the bells and whistles and video screens. Sandy became more involved with the church as time went on, and eventually ended up on their Finance Committee. I was now 74 and Sandy was 63 and this was just about all the activity we could handle.

In fact, it proved too much for me. In what was to become "June Swoon" for me over the next three years, I suffered a crush fracture of my L4 and L5 vertebrae while playing pickle ball. Sandy and I had taken up this "Senior friendly" game along with some neighbors, and were playing one morning in June when I ran backwards after the ball and fell backwards. My feet had caught in the surface causing the fall, and in an effort to protect my concussion prone head, I tucked my chin to my chest and took the full impact on my tailbone area. It turned out I was wearing the wrong type of shoes for the court surface. I wore running shoes when smoothed bottom tennis shoes were called for. Later that same day, another man did the exact same thing, but his fall resulted in surgery and a long convalescence.

I was assisted off the court and taken home, where no amount of Advil and red wine helped the pain. A trip to the emergency room resulted in pain pills and muscle relaxants, washed down with red wine, and a subsequent trip to the orthopedic surgeon resulted in the crush fracture diagnosis and a back brace. The red wine seemed to work because a few weeks later we left for our annual driving trip to California, with me laid out in the back of the Suburban on an air mattress. We survived that road trip and cabin "cleanup" without incident.

The next June, I was opening my father's day gift from Lauri on the front porch and reached for the box sitting on my left side and could not see my left hand or arm. I went blind from left to right like a shade was coming across my face. It lasted only a few minutes, but that was time enough for me to contemplate having totally blindness for the rest of my life. The process reversed itself slowly and I went into the house and told Sandy. It was a Sunday, but we called our ophthalmologist anyway and he actually responded. I thought it might have been my glaucoma acting up, but he thought it might be a minor stroke, or TIA, and had me come in the next morning. The whole thing cleared up within two hours, but he checked me out the next morning and recommended an MRI. When I went for the MRI, I found out I was claustrophobic and could not stay in the machine. They did a CT scan instead and the diagnosis was I had an age appropriate brain? I went down to Emory Hospital's Stroke Center for an evaluation, at Megan's urging, and they came up with a possible TIA.

Later that summer, we took Dana's eleven year old twin boys on a road trip from Soleil cross country to California. We stopped off in Memphis and stayed at the Peabody Hotel to see the ducks come down the elevator, from their rooftop house, and walk the red carpet to the fountain in the lobby. We later saw them walk back to the elevator and witnessed them come out on the roof and return to their house. Next stop was Hoover Dam and a third planned stop at the Indian Cliffside ruins of Mesa Verde never materialized because of inclement weather. We ended up with a week at our cabin near Yosemite, where their mother picked them up for the trip home to San Ramon. It was to be the last of our "togetherness sessions with the grandkids" before they got too old for that sort of thing.

About this time, Sandy decided it was "bucket list time" and booked us on an eleven day train trip across Canada and through the Canadian Rocky Mountains. My original bucket list item was to ride the Orient

Express in Europe, but found out the current trip lasted only four days on the train, and I wanted more time than that. Be careful what you wish for! We flew to Toronto and spent the night at the Fairmont Hotel. At check-in we received a complimentary drink ticket because Sandy had said it was our anniversary when booking the trip, which it was not. We decided to check out the "inexpensive" pub at the hotel for dinner and use the free drink ticket. I ordered a glass of champagne for Sandy on the free drink ticket and ordered a Manhattan for myself, while she went to the restroom, and found out when it arrived the cost of the Manhattan was $25.00. We did not have dinner at the Fairmont! We actually ate at a food truck on a street outside the hotel.

The train from Toronto to Jasper, Alberta, did not leave until the following night, so we had time to roam around Toronto. There was a baseball game that day at the stadium close by the hotel and the streets were full of Blue Jay fans decked out in the team colors arriving by train. The train station was across the street from the Fairmount. We observed several huge high rise condominiums in a row alongside the train station being built, and found out they were already pre-sold to Asian families. Also nearby was a multi-story space needle type structure with a rotating glass bottomed platform floor that looked over the city, and down into the baseball stadium. The ticket price for the ride up to the top was more than the price of admission to the baseball game.

We boarded the train that night and were escorted to our sleeping compartment that turned out to be a closet. The closet had pull-down bunk beds which, when down, allowed only enough room to walk sideways to the bathroom door. The bathroom (sink and toilet) was smaller than a commercial airline bathroom. When seated on the toilet, your nose almost touched the sink. To get up from the toilet, I had to grab the sink and work my shoulders up the walls on either side. There was a shower room in the passageway outside the compartment for the whole car. When the bunk beds were up, there was a single recliner type chair and a straight back wooden chair alongside the picture window. The only storage was a narrow space at ceiling level in the wall, reachable only from the top bunk. Sleeping was almost impossible! The wall from which the beds came out was now part of your sleeping arrangement, and also the wall between compartments. Our wall was defective and partially loose, to the extent we could hear the people in the next compartment moving about and talking. That, coupled with the side-to-side motion of the speeding train, made for an unpleasant evening.

The next morning we had breakfast in the dining car and found out there was an elevated domed observation car, to which you could escape your closet. Once there, however, we were asked to limit our time observing so others could enjoy the scenery. It turned out to be the only observation car on the train. Not to worry though, as the only scenery for the first three quarters of the trip was a tunnel of trees that topped off at the level of the observation bubble. We spent three miserable nights on that train. The trip across took that long because every once in a while we had to pull off on a siding to allow another train to pass us coming the other way. There was only one set of rails and they were privately owned with the commercial owner having the right of way.

We spent the night in Jasper and boarded a bus for a site seeing trip down to Banff, located in the southern tip of Alberta. On the way we stopped off at a glacier and were transported on to it by a huge tractor/gondola type vehicle and then turned loose to slosh around on the melting ice. At another stop we walked on a glass bottom walk-way that went out over a steep canyon. We also stopped at Lake Louise and toured a grand old Fairmount hotel. There are several big old Fairmount Hotels scattered throughout Canada, which we found out later were purchased by an Asian conglomerate. We spent two nights in Banff and took two trip sponsored tours, then boarded the Mountain Rocky Mountaineer magnificent train bound for Vancouver. Sandy had upgraded us for this leg of the trip and the service, accommodations, and food were exceptional.

The scenery through the Canadian Rockies was spectacular and our one night layover in Kamloops, British Columbia, was memorable as we were housed in what we thought was the bridal suite in the upscale hotel. It was a huge room with a large balcony overlooking the city, located in the very nice hotel with a fine dining restaurant. We were assigned to our own two level car on the train, with the upper level being domed from waist high and spacious seating for two. All alcoholic beverages were included and the Manhattans flowed all day. The lower section was the dining car where we enjoyed breakfast and lunch on a rotating basis. Half the upper car went down to the dining car to enjoy a gourmet meal while the other half on top were treated to snacks and cocktails until it was time to switch. The evening meal was provided at the five star hotel that we spent each night at. At the end, we spent two nights in Vancouver and, as before throughout this portion of the trip, we never had to handle our luggage, arrange transportation, or register at a hotel. Room keys were handed to you as you left the train and your luggage was waiting in your room when you arrived. Two interesting tidbits about Vancouver that we learned were that we could never afford to live there due to out-of-sight housing costs, and there was a four year window that required all tall buildings to have gardens on their rooftops.

Returning to my June Swoon story, the third June (of 2017) found me in the middle of a 45 day hospital stay that began with multiple trips to the ER with severe chest pain that I thought was heart related, but ended up with a diagnosis of hiatal hernia. It seems that many older people develop a widening of the small hole in the diaphragm that allows the esophagus to pass through and connect to the stomach. For some reason the stomach likes to see what is on the other side of the diaphragm and goes up through the widened hole, in some cases partially (acid reflux or heart burn), and in rare cases all the way through. I became one of the rare cases and my stomach ended up behind my heart. You might say I loved eating too much. In any case, the chest pains were really stomach pains and got progressively worse; to the point that surgery became a life-saving option. My primary care physician had told me to never have that surgery unless it became a life threatening situation, which it did, and I found his warning to be true.

Growing Old in America

The three hour, three small hole robotic surgery, with a three day hospital stay became a four and one half hour, five hole surgery with a 45 day hospital stay. My stomach had folded over on itself while sitting behind my heart, which added the two more holes and extra ninety minutes in surgery. The extra anesthesia time resulted in my entire digestive system going to sleep and not waking up. Thus a nasal gastric tube up my nose and down my esophagus into my stomach to drain stomach acids and eventually tube feed me. I had five or six IV's running all the time into my forearms, and both forearms eventually infiltrated and became swollen and unusable for any needle sticks. This necessitated a pic line up at my right clavicle that went directly into my heart. The pic line gave me clots in my right leg and my lung (pulmonary embolus). Because I could not take anything by mouth and my Sotolol heart pills did not come in IV form, I was given something else IV that put me in ICU twice before they figured out I was allergic to it.

I became the ten per cent man during that summer. Whatever they did or gave to me always had a ten percent chance of not working or going wrong, and it always did. I finally got out after 30 days and was doing fine until a severe bout of diarrhea put me back in with a bowel obstruction. I had lost 35 pounds during my 30 day vacation in the hospital, during which the mesh inguinal hernia repair I had done back in 2004 decided to perforate into my small bowel. The ten per cent rule kicked in following that surgical repair and the surgical wound in my umbilical cord became infected and extended my hospital stay to twelve days. A few days after that discharge, I was readmitted through the ER with severe diarrhea and a diagnosis of C-DIF, an intestinal infection that will stay with me the rest of my life, and a summer's worth of gastrointestinal problems. The wound infection lasted into October with Sandy performing caregiver, nursing, and transportation duties. I started out that summer as a young 77 year old (lots of compliments about looking younger than my age) and came out an old 78 year old. It was a miracle that I survived that summer and the year and a half that preceded it, but I did!

Walt Filkowski

The medical professionals said it would take almost a year before I approached any sort of normal body functions. Essentially one week for every day in the hospital, or 45 weeks. I managed to extend that time frame a bit with my next medical problem. We had gone to see our friendly Dermatologist every year to have the barnacles and other potentially harmful growths removed, and at the 2016 visit the good Doctor froze off a growth on my abdomen. This particular spot would not heal, but in view of my other string of medical problems that came up, it got lost in the shuffle. So, we missed the 2017 visit and when the end of 2018 came around, Sandy decided we needed to start up our annual dermatological check-ups again; particularly in view of the thing on my abdomen not healing. Of course the ten percent rule kicked in again and it turned out to be a Melanoma. Our daughter, Megan, got me in to see the head of Dermatology at Emory Medical Center, who later performed same day surgery to remove the now large and deep growth. They also took out lymph nodes from under both arm pits with the net result being a six inch scar across my abdomen and two and one half inch scars in my pits. Thus, my recuperation period was extended to just about a full year and Sandy got more practice in performing wound care.

During a follow-up visit two weeks later, the Dermatologists declared the Melanoma benign, but in examining me found another one on my right scapula. He suggested I allow him to take it out right then and there, rather than reschedule another surgical procedure somewhere down the line. I consented, but reconsidered when he asked the two residents in the room if they had ever seen the procedure done with a pair of scissors; the only surgical instrument he had in the exam room. It too was declared benign, but it left a two inch hole in my back.

After almost two years of my serious health problems, Sandy and I got a glimpse of what lay ahead of us in terms of growing even older together. Her role was going to be that of a care giver taking care of an older husband facing increasing physical deterioration. And, I have not even touched on Sandy's physical problems as she approached the age of 70.

The aging process is not kind to any aspect of the human body, and considerable time and expense is expended to defer and/or correct its effects. At the beginning of this epistle, I mentioned that one of the variables in growing old was how one took care of, or abused, his machine, or body. At my current age of 79 I will take the time to inventory the condition of the 79 year old machine I now reside in.

I will take this inventory from top to bottom, or head to toe, if you will. It is safe to say that most, if not all, of people my age of 79 will have experienced many of these problems. Any machine still running after 79 years is bound to have had some glitches, even with a good preventative maintenance program in place.

The head, as we know, houses the computer and is particularly vulnerable from both trauma and disease. In my case, trauma was an early issue with three LOC (loss of consciousness) concussions from 1956 through 1960 (sports related). Despite the recent attention given to football concussions (2018), I do not seem to have any related effects other than a rearranged nose and a slight speech impediment. A possible TIA in 2016 was determined to be a small blood clot that dissolved quickly, but left me temporarily blind, and a brain scan revealed an "age appropriate brain", whatever that is. An unusual result of these knocks to the noggin is my ability to hear my pulse inside my head. It sometimes got so loud I mistook it for machinery type noises. The noises first started at the Inn where we lived and slept in the basement, which contained the furnace, water heaters, walk-in freezer, and numerous pumps. I would get up at night in search of a malfunctioning something before finally realizing the noise was inside my head. It was sometime later that I figured out it was my pulse.

The head also houses four of the five senses, smell, taste, hearing and sight. Smell was not affected by the rearrangement of my nose, hearing has not been affected by lack of health care as a child and my mother's home remedies, but sight has been affected by some undetermined agent or occurrence. My eyesight had deteriorated by my freshman year in high school (20/300) for reasons unknown. Sitting too close to the television (12 inch screen) or genetics (I was the only one in a family of six needing glasses) did not seem to explain it. A cataract in one eye at age 45 was again unusual and unexplainable. The concussions and going blind temporarily from sunburned eyeballs while in the Navy were ruled out as possible causes. Then, a diagnosis of glaucoma following a lens implant for the cataract could never be explained. My other eye had a lens implant done at age 63. A suspected TIA in 2016 resulted in another bout of temporary blindness. The lens implants have corrected my vision to where I can function without glasses, but not optimally. I still experience "floaters", black spots, at times, but that comes with old age according to my ophthalmologist.

Being somewhat poor and without health or dental insurance as a child meant poor dental hygiene. Seeing a dentist meant having a tooth extracted and that was it. I never received dental care or performed dental care until joining the Navy at age 17. Despite poor dental hygiene, and losing a tooth playing hockey, I still have most of my teeth and wear a partial plate of only three teeth. I never had my tonsils out and they apparently just atrophied over time. My sense of taste has not been affected by any of the aforementioned; however my wife would argue that I never had any taste to begin with. At 79, I do still have a full head of hair and my brother did also when he died at age 82. I can attribute this to nothing other than red wine, to which I attribute most everything. I do now have a forward leaning head, or kyphosis, brought on by an aging arthritic cervical and thoracic portion of the spine.

The next thing in my bodily inventory is my trunk or thorax area extending from my neck down to my genital area. We already discussed my most recent stomach/intestine problem, but other problems started back in the Navy days at "A" school in Memphis when I had vague stomach pains that went undiagnosed because I did not want to interrupt my time there by reporting into sick bay. During my Navy days, I suffered an injury to my spine while surfing in California that left me temporarily paralyzed, and during my football days in college suffered two episodes of "hip pointers", where a blow to the iliac crest on the side crushes the muscle against the hip bone causing a massive painful hematoma. I also suffered two or three "stingers" playing football. These were hard blows to the front tip of the shoulder, usually occurring by tackling a ball carrier running directly at you, and leaving your arm temporarily paralyzed. They all occurred to my left shoulder and probably contributed to the acromioclavicular separation of the clavicle at my left shoulder while playing rugby some years later. Then came my early working days when a pilonidal cyst on my rectum would not heal and required a subsequent hemorrhoidectomy, which was possibly not necessary. This was followed a year later by a diagnosis of diverticulitis, and a strict diet that I only lasted a week on. The problem went away on its own and has never surfaced again. Another questionable diagnosis!

In my early fifties, I developed an enlarged prostate and flunked the PSI test. A bump biopsy turned up negative and ruled out cancer, but the prostrate continued to grow and I took medication until it finally closed off my ureter years later. At age 62 my gall bladder ruptured and they took it and my appendix out at the same time, as long as they were in the vicinity. A year later I had the first of two inguinal hernia repairs, this one on the left side. Then, at age 64, I had the big one; a cardiac event they now call it, and I wound up with a stent in one of the three large arteries in my heart.

After we sold the Inn and moved to Big Canoe, a few months after turning 65, my prostate finally closed off my ureter and I had the rotor rooter procedure, or TURP. At the same time, I had an inguinal hernia repair on the right side, but this time they used the mesh that caused me problems fourteen years later. I have had back problems off and on in my sixties and seventies and finally after a particularly bad back episode at age 70, I was evaluated at Emory University's spine center. Their final conclusion was that I had an "old back". The back got even older after a crush fracture of L4 and L5 while playing pickle ball at age 75.

Walt Filkowski

So, I found myself in my 70,s with an old back, an age appropriate brain, and a defective pump now slightly modified with a stent. Following my hiatal hernia multiple abdominal surgeries, I am left with a two handful s of blubber around my belly button which no one can explain. I am in otherwise fair physical condition with my 20 miles a week of walking, but have this abdominal "gut". That about sums up my trunk/thorax part of my body.

Next come the appendages, or arms, hands, legs, and feet. The first event was having a fish hook cut out of the ring finger of my right hand at age eight or nine, which coincidentally is the finger that has developed Dupree Syndrome in my 70's. This syndrome causes the tendon in the palm connected to the ring finger to tighten and pull the finger down into the palm. The first of my football injuries was a dislocated left elbow in my freshman year of high school. It became significant because the arm was left in a cast too long and the elbow lost 45 degrees of full extension permanently. Next came a partial tear of the right Achilles tendon from a football blocking sled, while in the Navy and playing football at a Junior College, at age 18. While in another junior college, after leaving the Navy, I fractured the Navicular bone in both wrists and dislocated my right thumb. By the time I quit playing football; I had dislocated various fingers numerous times and sprained/strained my ankles numerous times. My ankles are crisscrossed with numerous tiny blood vessels and veins from collateral circulation formed when the joints were swollen.

After transferring to a four year college, and in my 13th year of playing organized football, I suffered my first ever major knee injury, the "terrible triad". In growing up I had always walked long distances or rode a bike, and developed strong legs in doing so. Thus, thirteen years of football without a knee injury. In the triad injury, you essential dislocate your knee by doing almost a 360 degree turn at the knee with your foot planted. The three knee stabilizers to go are the medial collateral ligament on the inside of the knee, the inside cartilage in the knee joint, and the posterior cruciate ligament behind the knee. Without these three in place, the lower leg wiggles around in the wind. The inside collateral ligament was repaired with a piece of my saphenous vein, which no longer drains my lower right leg completely. The posterior cruciate ligament was reattached with cadmium screws, and the cartilage was removed, leaving me bone on bone on the inside of the knee.

The surgeon said that I would always walk with a limp, like the guy I replaced in the starting lineup, who suffered the same injury in preseason did. I rehabbed myself and played the next season, without a limp. Another injury to an appendage was a similar injury to my left knee playing flag football at age 39, but not as severe. Had the surgeon not died the day before surgery, it would have been operated on, but only for a cartilage tear. I agreed never to downhill ski or play flag football again to avoid surgery by the new surgeon. The most annoying of my dislocations occurred a week before my wedding to Sandy in 1981 and involved the little toe on my right foot. I hit my foot on a bed frame stored in a hallway and the dislocated toe, that now angled 90 degrees away from my foot, was reset by a clinic doctor with a pencil. I came down the aisle and danced at my wedding without one shoe and hobbled around Switzerland during our honeymoon.

Yet another appendage problem occurred sometime during our eight year tenure at the Inn. I had dropped a two horsepower electric motor on the big toe of my left foot and probably broke it, but hopped around on it for a few days until it quit hurting. I noticed the toenail turned black and then kind of sluffed off and was replaced by a whitish deformed nail. Over time all the toes on both feet became deformed except for the little toes on both feet. I referred to them as my wooden toenails. The local General Practice Doctor gave it some name and said it could be cleared up with a horribly expense medicine taken internally over a six month period…or then again not. As I was not yet on Medicare, I opted to live with it, and still do.

My final appendage problem to date occurred in Big Canoe in my early 70's, and involved a bite from a Brown Recluse spider on my left wrist. I apparently caught it early enough and a course of antibiotics prevented the tissue erosion that occurs with this type of spider bite. Lastly, my feet are worth mentioning, not because of injury, but because of their size. The length is not unusual, at ten and one-half; however the width has always been a problem at a triple E. I tell people I can water ski on my feet without water skis.

It seems that I tend to dislocate rather than fracture or break bones which, it turns out, is not a good thing. When you dislocate a joint, the tendons and ligaments get torn or stretched and this sometimes requires surgery and a prolonged recuperation period. In a break or fracture, only the bone itself is affected, a can often be reset with a closed reduction and not surgery. The only bones I have fractured are the small navicular bones in both wrists and the two lumbar vertebrae stress fractures. I dislocated an elbow, knee, nose, thumb, clavicle, and fingers and one toe. The dislocation of the clavicle from the scapula has left me with a bone spur at that junction, which is both painful and limits my range of motion at the shoulder. Just another old age ache/pain to put up with. The most amazing, and puzzling, skeletal issue is my right knee joint being bone-on-bone on the inside part of the joint since 1963, and not requiring a total knee procedure to date. My long list of back problems also include a water cyst in the first lumbar vertebrae that I never knew was there until an unrelated MRI discovered it while living in Big Canoe. There is nothing that can be done until it ruptures, so you live with it.

Lastly, the apparatus that holds everything in place and keeps out most infectious irritants is the epidermis, or skin, and I had been fortunate up until my late seventies in not having any major trauma to it other than surgical scaring. The only scar from trauma is on the inside of my left arm and resulted from the inside door handle penetrating that arm as a result of a car accident I had while in college. In growing up, I always had to get a good sunburn first thing every summer to start the tanning process. I continued this practice right on up to age 78, even after suffering from a squamous cell carcinoma behind my left ear at age 76. The following year my two melanomas appeared, thus ending anymore sunbathing! I still have a full head of hair, as already mentioned, and have always had hair on my forearms and lower legs. My mother used to say that hairy forearms were a sign of strength. Maybe that is why I do not have any hair on my chest. I seem to lack upper body strength that has resulted in many of my injuries. I prefer to think that my hairless chest is because hair does not grow on steel. The hair on my lower legs stops about eight inches up from my heel due to years of taping my ankles for football and pulling the hair follicles out when the tape was removed. Because I take the blood thinner Eliquis, I bruise easily and bleed more than usual from even the slightest scratch and clot slowly.

I have found that there are three major issues involved in the aging process; overall health, sex, and mental acumen. I have already covered the overall health issue and, while mental acumen is somewhat determined on certain aspects of overall health, I feel it is important enough to discuss separately. But first let me touch lightly on what is really important from the male perspective, and that is sex in old age. I say lightly because my wife is still around and embarrasses easily. As a result of my roto rooter procedure in 2004, at the age of 65, my active sex life began to go downhill. It was already on the downhill slide as a result of my ever enlarging prostate, but I was able to have erections and perform adequately, thanks in part to the little blue pill. Post roto rooter the ability to ejaculate became a problem, but erection was still in the cards. Intercourse was still occurring until the ripe old age of 74, and "then were none." Suffice it to say, that we still enjoy an occasional bout of sex at my age of 79, and leave it to your imagination.

Mental acumen is probably more important than we realize, for without it nothing else is possible. I am relatively with it at 79, with some memory loss both long distant and current. I do the recommended mental exercise of solitaire and crossword puzzle, play a lot of card and board games with neighbors, continuous reminisce with writing these books while walking, and drinking lots of red wine. As of late, I have experienced some episodes of what I refer to as "loss of awareness".

They usually occurred while driving, but the last one happened on one of my five mile walks, when I suddenly could not determine where I was or recognize my surroundings. Such episodes only last ten seconds or less, but are quite scary.

Suffice it to say, the end result of "all the above" is the older you get the more aches and pains you learn to live with. I still adhere to a "four day" rule that one of my football experiences taught me. Whenever I come up with an injury, ache or pain, or illness, I wait four days for it to heal or go away before seeing a Doctor.

FINAL DAYS IN SOLEIL

It is now October of 2018 and we have lived in Soleil about four and one half years. We have settled into a routine of sorts with Sandy and me sometimes doing our own thing and sometimes doing things together. She cooks and I do the dishes. We split housecleaning duties until finally breaking down and hiring someone to do it after my prolonged hospital stay in 2017. I take care of the cars and most of the yard work and Sandy does the rest of the inside domestic chores and finances. I wash windows and she paints. Life in old age becomes more of a partnership and less of a relationship.

One thing about an over 55 active adult community is there is always something to do. Whether or not you choose to do it is entirely up to you. Some households choose to do nothing or very little because of age or health issues, or because they simply do not care to participate. We limit our participation now mostly to our 34 house pod, and play monthly games of Mexican Train dominoes, euchre, poker, bunco, Mah Jong, and pick-up games of hand-and-foot. We have a monthly geographical dinner group of ten couples living close together on our street, with each couple choosing a restaurant for the group to go to. There is an annual Octoberfest celebration in our Pod and we do an annual Christmas Party for the Pod. We attend a Christmas Luncheon, Super Bowl party, Valentine Day dinner, and New Year Eve party within the Pod each year and attend several clubhouse events with other neighbors. Sandy volunteers one day a week at MUST MINISTRIES in Canton and sits on our church finance committee, and I play golf at least once a week with a group of old guys, The Hackers, as weather permits. Like most seniors (but not all), I do not play in the rain, or when it gets below fifty degrees. Neither Sandy nor I like to drive at night anymore, and daytime activity outside the gates is mostly limited to church, doctor and dentist appointments, shopping and dining. With the exception of medical visits to Emory in Atlanta, most trips outside the gates are within ten miles.

Walt Filkowski

We were fortunate when moving to Soleil in 2014 to be moving into a newly built- out pod of 32 homes, in which we were the third occupants. We got to know each new couple as they moved in, and already knew three couples that we had recruited from Big Canoe. It was helpful that we all shared common construction problems and reached out to each other in search of dentists, physicians, etc. Sandy baked each new resident in our pod a loaf of her bread, which helped break the ice. Five years later we live in a neighborhood of friends that help each other out when needed. My golfing buddy Bob, who lives across the street and kept my golf game alive when I was about to give up by teaching me the "Bob Swing", also makes the best Manhattan I have experienced. I have developed a liking for Manhattans, in addition to red wine, and Bob always makes doubles. Sandy is the knitting Guru of the neighborhood and offers advice and mentoring for the ladies.

We are both walkers and do two to three miles almost every morning. I have built up my walking over the past year to five miles three days a week, for a total of twenty miles weekly, as part of my recuperation from the previous year's hospitalization. Sandy is a Fitbit fanatic and has to do 10,000 steps a day or she declares the day a failure. I have found that my length of stride has shortened considerably over the years, due partly from my knee injuries that lost full flexion and extension of both lower legs, but mostly from old age. I now walk with shorter steps and hunched slightly forward, a typical "old age gait." It is not the "nursing home shuffle" yet, but not too far from it.

I do a lot of sitting out on the back patio in the afternoons with a glass or two of wine with Oliver our dog. We have country/western or 50's music on and I reminisce about the good old days. Oliver surpassed me this year in age (dog years) and is now the elder statesman of the household. We watch the birds that come to drink and bathe in our small waterfall, or chow down at the bird feeders. If you had told me fifty years ago that I would ever be sitting around watching birds, I would have written you off as being crazy. A pair of big red cardinals come twice a day to feed, and a bunch of humming birds are kept at bay by a pair of hummers that took ownership of the hummingbird feeder in the spring. Our trees and shrubs in the yard, that we mostly had put in four years ago, in a mature state, have fully grown out and keep me busy trimming and fertilizing. It is now my main hobby since I can no longer work with my outdoor train layout.

Sandy and I have talked about the future off and on since my poor health year of 2017, and never came up with a viable plan. We have a problem that is somewhat unique to couples our age, but not all that unique, in that Sandy is nine years younger than me. While I am 79 and fading fast, she just turned 70 and is going strong. I am on a ship that is slowly sinking and Sandy is just sailing along. We recently attended a session at Lanier Village in nearby Gainesville, a life care center where you enter as independent living residents and progress through the assisted living, skilled nursing or memory care living, and long term care, as needed. Essentially, you are there for the rest of your life, as once accepted they can never kick you out. We had almost placed Sandy's father in this facility some years ago when we lived in Big Canoe, but he cancelled out when his supposed East Coast girlfriend refused to accompany him. It is a place I am ready for, but Sandy is not.

The burning issue is that both parties have to be completely independent to get accepted. In my present condition, I could lose that independence at any time and not be eligible for that type facility. After the Lanier Village session and further discussion, we agreed that we should go on the waiting list for Lanier Village. However, later Sandy decided she was just not ready for a commitment to spend the rest of her days in a living arrangement far away from her daughters and other family members, or give up what she has now in our present situation in Soleil. She is adamant about personally caring for me when I become infirmed, in spite of my being adamant about that never happening. I do not want her spending her remaining time taking care of me. Our most recent compromise over this dilemma is to wait two years until Megan finishes her post-doctorate experience in Houston, and see where she ends up. The problem with that is there never is an "end" to where your kids go and you end up chasing your kids, an all to frequent occurrence among seniors and one we said we would never do again. Sandy's daughter, Lauri, moved from Livermore, California, to Peachtree City, to Australia, back to Peachtree City, and then back out to California. The last three moves within a four year period!

Our blended family's four children are now in, or approaching, middle age and have experienced some of the same problems that Sandy and I have faced over the years. Dana, now 49, divorced after twenty years of marriage and is a single mom to teenage twin boys. Lauri, also 49, is dealing with a recovering alcoholic husband and a transgender child. Megan, at age 34, is divorced and has the distinction of having been married and divorced in the same court house. My son, Scott, and I have somewhat reconciled after seventeen years of not communicating. At 47 he is still attempting to "game the system" with workers comp and total disability lawsuits. He has hooked up with a very nice lady and her son and daughter, for an instant family situation without the complications of marriage. We met up in the summer of 2018 at my grandson's graduation from middle school in California, and had breakfast the following morning. Later that summer, I gave him my Forty-Niners jacket, as he remains a "Niner" fan. He will always blame me for screwing up his life with the divorce from his mother, and that will never change no matter what I do. He has always adored Sandy and once told her that if I was not around he would be on her "like flies on honey." He is contemplating a move to Oregon with his new family, if he wins his workers comp and total disability lawsuits.

Earlier that year, in April, I decided to attend San Francisco State University's Football Hall of Fame Banquet because I thought one of my close friends on that team was being inducted and several other old teammates were going to be there. I flew out and back over a weekend and the trip was both rewarding and sad. It was great to see some old faces, but disheartening to see the physical condition of some and to learn of the deaths of still others. The two most physical specimens I had ever played with, or against, had fallen victim to Parkinson's and Alzheimer's disease, and were mere shells of themselves. Though three to four years older than my teammates, because of my military service, I was in better physical and mental health than most, but saw the handwriting on the wall.

In May of 2018, Megan received her PhD. in Neuroscience from Georgia and we helped her move to Houston to begin her Post Doc at Baylor University Research Center. She and her significant other, David, loaded up a U-Haul truck in Athens and drove to Soleil, where her sister, Lauri repacked it and added the stuff of Megan's we had stored in our attic. I drove the truck to Houston and Megan and Sandy followed with Megan's dog and other junk in the Cadillac. On the way home from Houston, we stopped in Mobile, Alabama, to have lunch with one of my high school buddies I had graduated with sixty-one years ago. While still in pretty good shape, he did have the beginnings of a tremor in one arm.

In late June, we flew out to California to attend the twin grandson's graduation from Junior High School, and I connected with my son, Scott, after seventeen years of not communicating. We also drove up to Santa Rosa to visit our former residence and neighborhood of million dollar homes that were burned to the ground. Of over one hundred homes in the development, maybe five were still standing. One was less than twenty yards from our burned out former home. We then spent five days with Lauri's family in Nevada City, near Lake Tahoe, before flying home.

We finished out that summer with a one month " bucket list" road trip from Georgia to, and through, California visiting all the "old haunts" and friends and family. Billed as "the last of the road trips", the three of us (Oliver got to go on this trip) drove from Georgia to Denver to visit the nieces (my brother had died the year before at age 82), then on to Reno to see a former work friend we had not seen in twenty-two years. From there it was a short haul to drop off Oliver at Lauri's in Nevada City, and then North to the Benbow Inn, the original Inn we tried to buy three times up near the Oregon border, that no longer took dogs. We left the Benbow and drove down Highway 1 on the coast, passing the spot the woman drove off into the ocean with her entire family, and into Mendocino, where we visited and stayed at Inns we had thought about buying during our Inn search. We passed through the coastal town of Gualala, where my first wife now resides, but elected not to pay her a visit. One could only carry "friends and family" so far. We continued down the coast past San Francisco to Pacifica, where we had dinner at the Moonraker restaurant on the beach; a restaurant where I was first introduced to Abalone some fifty years ago. Then on to visit family in Cambria, near Hearst Castle, friends in Aptos, near Santa Cruz, and on into Monterey, where we had an Abalone dinner at the Sardine Factory, at $91.00 a serving. Needless to say, we split a serving.

The drive back up north to Lauri's to retrieve Oliver took us through Cupertino, on the San Francisco Peninsula, to visit my two remaining college roommates, up to the San Ramon Valley to visit Dana and the twins, then on to Nevada City and Oliver. From Nevada City we drove south to the cabin for a week of maintenance and preparedness to put it on the market. This was to be my last trip to the cabin as the maintenance was getting to be too much. The drive back to Georgia included a stopover outside of Dallas, Texas, to visit old friends from Big Canoe, and a diversion down to Houston to see Megan. In all, we drove 7200 miles and were gone five weeks.

It is now the Christmas Season of 2018 and I am about four months on my way to being eighty years old. I can hardly say it, let allow envision being it. Megan became engaged on Thanksgiving Eve and much to our amazement began talking about future children. We had always agreed with her former premise that she was not suited to child rearing. This further complicates our dilemma about where are next move will be. Megan announced a November of 2019 wedding date and selected a mountain wedding up in Blue Ridge, about ninety minutes north of our home in Soleil.

Every year about this time we write a Christmas Letter to our longtime friends scattered across the country detailing the trials and travels of the Filkowski clan over the past year, instead of sending a Christmas card. We limit it to friends and specifically exclude family because we have always been up front and humorous about our family. I used to write the letters, but turned that function over to Oliver (Megan's Chihuahua that came to live with us in 2005), in 2007. In this year's letter, Oliver observes that Papa Walt and Momma Sandy have Nomadic tendencies, in that they tend to relocate every five to nine years since getting married in 1981, and even did so before their marriage, in other lives. Since 1981 it was nine years in Danville, California, five years in Santa Rosa, eight years at the Inn in Mercersburg, Pennsylvania, and nine years in Big Canoe, Georgia. As they approach five years here in Soleil, Oliver states he has observed them discussing a possible relocation back to California.

An opportunity has presented itself for a possible move to Lompoc, California, on the Central Coast. Sandy's ex-father-in-law, whom she was, as still is, close to, has moved into a nursing home at age ninety-nine and his fifty-year old house is available. All parties concerned would like to see Sandy in that house in the future. She knows the house, as does her daughter and his granddaughter, and what it would take to make it happen financially. Nothing will happen until the old gentleman passes, but it is a possibility and a solution to a final move for us, and particularly Sandy.

A few months after writing the above, February 26th to be exact, we flew out to California to look at the old Lompoc house, and to escape another cold Georgia winter for a week. To fill in the week, we decided to revisit the Palm Springs area site (Del Webb in Indio) where we were having a house built in 2013, and the Paso Robles over- fifty-five gated community that we liked, but could not afford (only 30 minutes from Sandy's brother). We found a house in Indio we liked and could afford, and a house in Paso Robles we liked, but could not afford. Same scenario as in 2013! The decision on which area to live in changed day-to-day. We asked Megan if San Diego (closer to Indio) was still in her plans, and she announced that she and her soon-to-be husband had just applied to the National Health Institute in Washington, D.C. and the CDC in Atlanta. Great…we move to the west coast and Megan ends up back East again! Also, Sandy began lamenting about Megan getting married back in Georgia in nine months, which created a logistics problem were we to move west in the near future. There was also a question of what if our house in Soleil would sell for a decent price, following a botched sale of our same model two houses down from us that lowered the real estate comps for our area considerably. We finally decided, after a week of back and forth, to wait a year and see if the comps came back up, and see where Megan may finally end up. So much for never following your kids! We also placed ourselves on the waiting list at Lanier Village, the life care facility in Gainesville, as a back-up plan.

Growing Old in America

LIFE BEGINS AT EIGHTY

Fast forward to the late summer of 2019 and pick up life in Soleil. As I approached the big 8-0, my daughter, Dana, turned fifty on the same day. She threw herself a 50th birthday party at a winery in Livermore, California, and invited us to attend. We declined the invitation, as Sandy had planned to fly out in October to close down the cabin and straighten up a bit for a possible sale and I had paid my last visit up there sometime back. After some soul-searching discussion involving my longevity, with the age of 80 around the corner and family, we decided to secretly fly out and surprise her at the party, provided I agreed to go up to the cabin one more time.

Lauri was invited to the 50th bash, much to our surprise as the step-sisters had not really connected much over the years. Even more surprising was that she and her husband, Kevin, were coming down from the Lake Tahoe area for the event and then coming up to the cabin to help with the maintenance. We flew into Oakland the Thursday night before the Saturday afternoon affair, and visited Sandy's ex-husband for lunch in Aptos, on the coast. Sandy's ex, Al, has been opening and closing the cabin the last several years in exchange for staying there whenever they wanted, but were opting out of that arrangement. We were supposed to have dinner with Lauri and her husband Friday night, but they cancelled in favor of dining with some long lost old neighbors from their old neighborhood in Livermore.

Lauri and Kevin drove down from Nevada City in his backwoods Jeep because they were coming up to the mountain cabin, so we drove separately out to the winery. The event started at noon and we arrived about that time and parked our rental car in an inconspicuous spot away from the action, and snuck in from the back. We were spotted by the sixteen year old twins, who it turned out were in on our secret appearance, and they took us up to their mom and turned her around to see us. Dana was genuinely surprised and elated to see us there and that made the trip worthwhile. A little later, Sandy and I were inside the winery looking at some artwork and Sandy said it would be perfect if Megan could have come from Houston and the three daughters there. She no longer got the words out of her mouth when someone tapped on her shoulder and it was Megan. Sandy let out a scream that was probably heard in Georgia. So now all three daughters were together for the first time in many moons. Megan make an off-hand comment about that not being all the surprises coming that day, and a little later my son, Scott, and his significant other showed up. This was the first time all four of the "his, hers, and ours" had been together in twenty-two years.

It turned out that Lauri and Kevin cancelled dinner with us on Friday night to have dinner with Megan and her finance, David; and Megan had breakfast with Scott on Saturday morning and talked him into coming to Dana's party, which he had already responded no to. Things went so well at the party that we all agreed to have dinner together that night to celebrate my 80th birthday. Dinner went so well that we all agreed to have breakfast the next morning. To top it all off, everyone agreed to come to Megan's wedding in Georgia in November. All of a sudden we were a family again! That afternoon we all scattered off again in the wind. Lauri and Kevin and Sandy and I to the cabin, Megan and David back to Houston, Scott in a few weeks up to Oregon, where he purchased a home with his settlement money (another story), and Dana and the twins back to work and school, respectively.

In retrospect, it would appear that age might have something to do with families coming back together. My brother and I came back to our two sisters late in life, and my son seems to have reestablished a relationship with his sisters as well as Sandy and I, as he approaches the age 50 milestone. My approach to, and reaching, eighty seems to have changed my outlook on family, for the better according to Sandy. Before I get off the subject of my reaching eighty years of existence on this planet, I need to state for the record that my wife of 38 years (as of this writing) gave me an all-time birthday present that topped what she did for me on my 40th, 50th, 60th, and 70th birthdays; and which surpassed everything on my bucket list. Unfortunately, censorship protocol prevents my mentioning what the present was.

    I now consider myself to be old! That saying about sixty being the new forty is a lot of nonsense. Eighty is old! Aside from the physical and mental deterioration, my biggest problem is dealing with change. As a result, I have become very cynical, or at the very least, skeptical of how life, as we are currently experiencing it now, is progressing. Webster defines cynical as being scornful of the motives or virtues of others, and skeptic as one who doubts, questions, or disagrees with generally accepted assertions. When around people our age you hear a lot about "how it used to be" and "the good old days, when....", or "things are sure different now". I am sure each generation felt the same way about the generation before it, and I know my parents and my friends parents thought rock and roll would be the undoing of my generation. However, social media, television, and the media in general have altered life, not only in this country, but globally. I believe we have seen more change in the past twenty-five years than in the fifty years that preceded the early 1990's.

    I could go on for pages about changes I have witnessed in my lifetime, but here are a few that push my button and has turned me into a cynic. Some are the result of the media and their perception that the American public has a need to be constantly entertained. Actually, forget the perception part. I believe Americans would like to be entertained seven-twenty-four, if it could be done while they are sleeping. Professional sports have become pure entertainment and its superstars have become prima donna's, interested more in making money and achieving notoriety than in the game itself. American politics are not only a joke, but a real concern to the future of this country. Harry Truman was the last President to not have had a scandal in his term of office, and now even political debates have become entertainment, thanks to the media. Life itself has become entertainment as seen in the advent of "reality shows", with ridiculous plots involving dwarfs, severely overweight people, and the sex-laden

"Housewives of ...." series. I have witnessed the transition of the morning or evening thirty minute news into three to four hour presentations by five people, all talking at the same time and including the correct political mix of white and black, and male and female. The "news" now includes sports, weather, traffic, health, "pop news", human interest features, and endless commercials. Hollywood has run out of original scripts and turn out sequels of any movie that turned a profit initially. They also turn out "remakes" on a regular basis. I have seen three remakes of King Kong since the original in 1939. I suppose this could be a drawback of living too long.

Hollywood has also become politicalized, particularly as of late, since Trump was elected President. I suppose their liberal anti-government sentiments date back to the McCarthy communist witch-hunting days during the 1950's, when many of them were blacklisted. The female contingent has really come out firing with the advent of the Me-Too movement. Professional sports athletes, both male and female have also jumped on the bandwagon, thanks to the media, and have an opinion on just about everything.

At poker games, we men jokingly said woman are taking over the world, but in reality that may not be far off. Woman have come a long way in the last ten years, to their credit and long overdue. In my opinion, however, it is approaching over-kill in terms of the speed with which they have come so far. Entertainment enters into this, as men, in particular like a pretty face; and there are a lot of pretty faces on sports talk shows, interviewing players at half-time, and even in the locker room surrounded by half-naked men post-game. Just this morning it was reported (by the usual unofficial sources) on T.V (therefore it must be true) that women country/westerns singers protested at one of the multi entertainment award shows that occur around the first of each year, that c/w radio stations refuse to play female records back-to-back. Another earth shattering protest! As of this writing, of the top twenty-five books on Amazon's kindle, all but two our authored by women., and most of the story line is about women! How did this happen?

It is now November of 2019 and we have survived Megan and David's wedding at the mountain retreat outside of Blue Ridge, Georgia. The good news is that it was another family event, even an extended family event with the addition of Sandy's grandson and granddaughter being present. This proved to be a Sandy production all the way and she outdid herself, as usual. She helped the caterer with the rehearsal and wedding dinners and cooked four meals for twenty to thirty people herself. She also baked the multi-tiered wedding cake and set it up, in addition to the usual mother-of-the-bride duties. Decorating duties fell to her with the items she made for the function. As a result, she missed most of the socialization and some of the function itself.

The bad news is more of concern than of disappointment. The rehearsal itself never happened, because it got too late with all the drinking and people arriving late, or not at all. The outdoor wedding was unique, to say the least, with the minister being a female friend ordained via internet giggling, along with the bride and groom, through the ceremony. The shocker was the pronouncement of the bride and groom as Mr. and Mrs. Frankowski (a combination of the groom's last name of Frank with the bride's last name of Filkowski). We had heard this discussed some time ago as a joke, not as reality, and sort of assumed such at the wedding. Unfortunately, it has proven to be reality. Our concern became one of the event being just one big party, an expensive one at that, with no thought for tradition or the parents (who were essentially ignored until something had to be done). The underlying issue was the drinking. I am not one to be concerned, as I did my share, but signals came out that the generation present had some problems.

Prior to the wedding, Megan had applied for, been vetted, and hired by the National Institute of Health, in spite of her somewhat suspect father, yours truly. In a six or seven week time period, she closed down her programs at Baylor, met with her new people at NIH, researched and purchased a house in Maryland, and packed and drove a U-Haul truck to the new house and moved in. Her new hubby, David, quit his research Post-Doctoral position at MK Anderson Hospital in Houston to join Megan. He has applied to the National Institute of Health for three separate positions so far, but to no avail. He is keeping busy working at his favorite thing, making and serving beer at a brewery.

Fast forward again to February of 2020! My neighbor Bob from across the street has reminded me that I have lived in ten generations beginning with the 1930's (born in 1939). Life goes on as usual in Soleil. I celebrate Halloween by dressing up in ghoul costume from head to foot and wear a sign around my neck that reads "trick or wine". I do not speak and was recognized for the first couple of years, but the wine request eventually gave me way. We had our annual Christmas Party again and, as usual, Sandy has declared "never again". She might be right this time, as three previously scheduled events this time of year in our neighborhood were not held this year, and there is talk of the big fall Octoberfest event may not be held this coming fall. It could be we are all getting older or health issues are becoming more prevalent.

On the first of January, the Developer turned over the community to our own HOA, and the fun began. We went through this process while living in Big Canoe and know what is coming. To complicate things, the Developer and the Advisory Board decided to change management companies during 2019 and this has proven to be a disaster. The Developer has not finished building out yet and still has a seat on the new HOA Board. His shoddy construction practices still haunt him as almost all of his homes need to be repainted after three to four years and the current issue is the hardy-plank concrete board siding cracking after the same time period. In spite of the shoddy construction, however, Soleil has proven to be a good choice as an active adult community, and becoming harder and harder to leave as we move up the waiting list for Lake Lanier Village. We are six to eight weeks away from reaching the top of the list, as of February of 2020.

PANDEMIC

It is now April of 2020 and, after only four months of this notable calendar year, it might become the most memorable year of my eighty so far. The year began with a new strain of flu showing up in China in January and spreading to other countries rapidly. It was flu season, and with a global economy this was not unusual. What was different was the high death rate, particularly among the elderly and people with pre-existing severe health issues. Add to this mix the internet and social media and the result was world-wide panic. The news media did their usual exploitation and blew the situation into a world-wide crisis. The virus, now called Covid-19, did not really show up in this country until March, and the news media went ballistic. The issue became politicized and the Democrats, whose campaign to denigrate Trump was sagging, used the "pandemic" to blame the Administration for either doing too little or too much to address the situation here in the United States.

Despite the fact that some 80,000 died from the Flu in 2019 in the U.S. and we were only at half that amount by mid-April, the media did their thing and we ended up with "social distancing" and "shelter in place"; two new sayings to add to our ever-growing vocabulary. By June the virus seemed to have run its course and the country began to open back up, led by Georgia. I did not believe it was anything more than a flu epidemic, similar to those in the past, and blown out of proportion by the media. I researched it on Google and found that approximately 8800 people died each day in the U.S. and that figure remained constant for the same twelve month periods during 2019 and 2020. What did change was the increase in deaths attributed to the Covid virus for the 2020 period. However, there was a corresponding decrease in pneumonia and flu deaths, which resulted in no increase in deaths overall. When I tried to find that web site again later, it was no longer available. The fact that Medicare paid around $13,000 for a Covid diagnosis to hospitals, in addition to whatever diagnosis a patient had (which most likely killed them), may have inflated the death rates and Covid cases for people over age 65.

The county we live in, Cherokee County, has not been impacted by the virus even close to the three counties comprising the greater Atlanta Area, and our now 900 home community of Soleil has only experienced four cases through July of 2020. Other states in the U.S. did not fare as well as Georgia, and California and New York were impacted severely. The San Francisco Bay Area put in a "shelter in place" mandate and people were not allowed out except for "essential" reasons, including no walks or bike riding. Because Dana was considered "law enforcement" in her job as a Deputy District Attorney, she was considered "essential" and not subject to "sheltering in place". Being an avid bike rider, Dana decided to go for a bike ride in a nearby community, which nearly cost her life. While cycling down a hill at about 30 mph, she encountered a dead animal on the roadway being eaten by large vultures. Her arrival on the scene caused the big birds to panic and take flight. Unfortunately, one flew into Dana causing a high impact accident. Dana ended up with a fractured skull and a brain bleed, and ended up in a trauma center. She also suffered a broken clavicle, among other severe bumps and abrasions, but this could not be repaired at the time because elective surgery was not being performed due to overcrowding from the virus pandemic.

Repair of the clavicle occurred some weeks later, but this delayed repair resulted in the clavicle separating from its connection at the shoulder and required another surgery over a month later. Dana's brain bleed resulted in a speech impediment and seizures, which took away her driving license for six months. There was some concern about how all of this would affect her previous brain tumor involving the optic nerve, but everything worked, out thanks to Sandy's (and a lot of other people's) prayers. Dana returned to work within a few months with no long term effects.

The sheltering in place phenomena begin to wear thin and people began to ignore the mandate and gather in clusters, or bubbles of family members or neighbors you knew were practicing safe measures. In our

Trentonville section of 34 homes, there were three such "bubbles". The one we participated in had six couples, all who lived within 50 yards of each other. We sit around a circle outdoors maintaining a six foot distances, and have a cocktail or two while solving or complaining about world problems. That worked for a while then became less frequent and finally stopped, as people began to travel or were laid up with physical problems requiring surgery or other hospitalizations.

Anyway, it did not take long for the media to lose interest in the Pandemic and jump on the "social justice" bandwagon. The killing of African-Americans by law enforcement members, some of which are African-Americans, while apprehensible, is nothing new. Having lived and worked in and around Oakland, California for thirty-five years where African-Americans constituted 65 percent of the population, I witnessed the Black Panther movement during the 1970's, which is strangely similar to the "Black Lives Matter" movement and resulting riots and civil unrest that has resulted in 2020. The only difference this time around is the media coverage. The media loves to cover riots and civil unrest, and people love to see themselves performing these criminal acts. In a great example of people getting what they deserve, the Covid flu epidemic appeared to be on the decline before the large-scale protests and rioting, but some fourteen days (the incubation period) later it went back on the rise.

By June everyone was becoming "stir crazy" with sheltering in place and looking for things to do. My outlet was posting humorous signs in our front lawn. I played off the pandemic itself with signs like "Will wash your hands for food" and "Slightly used masks for sale". We have a lot of walkers from both inside and outside Trentonville come through our pod and past our yard because the streets are relatively flat, and for the most part they enjoyed the signs. When I walked my five miles, other walkers would stop me and comment on the signs. When I posed a sign that read "clothing optional", my neighbor behind us hung a pair of his underwear on it. That apparently offended someone and the HOA gave me two weeks to "cease and desist" or incur a fine. My neighbors were upset over this and plotted ways to continue the practice, but cooler heads prevailed and life when on as the "new normal".

I was not done, however, and when the fourth of July came around I was ready. About four years previous, someone started a golf cart parade inside Soleil, with the golf carts decorated in patriotic fashion. It never really took off and had only four or five golf carts that travelled a short route mainly along the main streets. But in the year of the Pandemic, boredom was at its peak, and the parade took on major proportions. "Sheltering in place" guaranteed a larger audience and much more participation. I love a good parade, a la the Mercersburg Halloween parade, and rallied my animals to express my feelings. I lined up all the stuffed, ceramic, and plastic animals we had accumulated over the years on our large three-car driveway to view the parade. I think there were about 25 critters cheering on the parade, and we actual stopped the procession a few times when people stopped their golf carts to take pictures.

In late July, we found out the October San Francisco State University Football Hall of Fame induction ceremony luncheon that had been cancelled in April was again cancelled, with plans to do a "virtual" induction. They had finally run out of former players to induct, and I had been tapped. By October I will be 81 years old and probably the oldest player ever inducted. It only took 56 years since my last year of playing in 1964. As background, I had to write up some memories of my playing days and teammates, and I responded that there were probably not any players, coaches, media, or former students left who would know what I was talking about.

Again, in late July we decided to challenge the shelter in place mandates and travel up to Maryland to visit our youngest daughter Megan and her new husband and new house. Some of the Northeast states had posted certain other states as "persona non grata" and Georgia was one of the states they did not want visitors from. Fortunately, Maryland was not one of these paranoid states, nor was Pennsylvania where we visited our former Inn while up in the area. We spent six nights with Megan and her husband, with one night at our former Inn in Mercersburg, PA. The visit to the Inn was disheartening as the two subsequent owners had let the five acres of expensive landscaping we had installed turn to weeds and overgrowth, or in some cases removed entirely. Sandy was very disappointed with the changes made to the interior and the fact some of the bedding and linens we purchased some 20 years ago were still being used. We spoke with our former manager and another former employee we visited in town and they echoed our disappointment with the property. We also learned that Police Chief Larry had died, that the "chicken wing restaurant had changed hands, and that the "Romanian terror restaurant had sold, but never reopened. The "Bates Motel" B&B in town became a residence once again, and the Chevrolet dealer where I purchased our first Suburban had become a large cheap gas/fast food establishment. Nothing stays the same, even in small town America.

While up North we also visited another life care Facility close to Silver Springs where Megan lives. An idea that Sandy had was when I finally pass, she decided that Megan was the daughter she most likely needed to live closest to. Megan's husband, David, had also been hired by the Health Institute of America and the two PhD's were working at home. Their short-lived flirtation with having children was abandoned in favor of careers and lifestyle, and their child substitutes became two large dogs. On the drive home from this visit, Sandy ruled out this option for a variety of reasons.

As I approached the age of 81 in a couple of weeks, in the middle of a never-ending Pandemic, I am faced with the problem of how to end this epistle. It has indeed become more of a diary that a biography and not of much value as such. I am still growing old and listing all the health related issues becomes redundant, and probably boring to the reader. My neighbor Bob, of the "Bob Swing" and Manhattan fame, is on my case to finish up and get this thing published so he can read it. I am caught in a dilemma of; is this all there is going forward and time is running out, or is there still more to come and I should stick it out until I cannot write anymore.

    I have endured my 81st birthday and Sandy went all out again on this one within the limited scope of the pandemic. She had me do a scavenger hunt to find the gifts she had hidden throughout the house. There were little gifts of socks and chocolates, but the big gift was a Roomba, the computer robot floor cleaner. My weekly chore was dusting and vacuuming, and it had gotten so I had to wear a back brace to push the big Dyson vacuum around 2700 square feet of floor space. The Roomba is amazing and temporarily broke up the boredom of "living in place". Sandy also made banana fritters soaked in a white chocolate and crème ingles sauce for breakfast, and made a cocoanut crème pie (my favorite) for desert after dinner out at a restaurant. She has outdone me again on birthdays.

    I have contacted the publisher of my last book he did in 2013, and was happily surprised to find out the cost would be about the same this time around. So much for inflation! The problem is where and when to end the damn thing. I had hoped by now to be in a place where I would have lived out my remaining productive time, but apparently this is not to be when married to someone nine years younger than you and very active. Sandy is still committed to taking care of me at home, if and when that time comes, in spite of my insistence that will never happen. The battle rages on! Perhaps there could be a sequel book "Growing Older in America".

    I hate to bring up another health issue but, the lens implant I had done at age 45 failed and floated around the eye, sometimes going up on top of the eyeball. If it got behind the eyeball itself it could damage the retina, so a procedure to remove the wandering lens and insert a new one was performed stat. The problem was the wandering lens was rigid and a larger hole had to be made to get it out, as opposed to the small hole needed for the modern flexible lens that could be inserted folded and then opened up. The other problem was the new lens could not go where the old lens had been because the tissue to which a lens would be attached had eroded. The new lens was placed outside the old location, but still inside the eyeball. It was attached with something akin to rivets, per the ophthalmologist. The result was learning to live with the feeling of something being in your eye due to a stitch needed to close the larger hole and the "rivets" needed to attach the new lens. It took about eight weeks to get used to this new normal.

Another interesting malady occurred a week ago involving an electric shock pain in my right ankle that began in bed at two a.m., and continued every five to ten seconds thereafter. The electrical jolt would cause my hold body to jump. I mention this only because it was so unique, and a puzzle to the physician who examined me. X-rays were negative and he prescribed a cream to rub on the ankle and Lyrica pills to reduce the whole body reaction. The Lyrica provided the best night's sleep I had for years; seven to eight hours of uninterrupted glorious sleep. If there were not so many possible side effects, I would take it every night. The pain cleared up in four days and has not come back.

Walt Filkowski

THE END OF THE BOOK (NOT ME)

I have decided to end this thing here; two weeks after my 81st birthday and fully ambulatory with only occasional atrial fib, some melanomas, glaucoma, bone spur on left shoulder, two crushed vertebrae in lumbar spine, water cyst in lumbar vertebrae, and some post abdominal surgery complications. Missing body parts include the appendix, gall bladder, eye lenses, small amount of small intestine, and most of prostate. Age-related repairs include two inguinal hernia repairs and a hiatal hernia repair. Implants include a heart stent and a cadmium screw in my right knee. I mention all this because it is what growing old means….your parts wear out! I did not include injuries incurred in my younger days. Mentally I am twenty-one and can leaped off tall buildings, but physically all I can do is fall off of tall buildings; and there are some days I contemplate doing just that. I still walk twenty miles a week and play nine holes of golf once, sometimes twice, a week. Getting up from sitting and bending over and straightening up is painful. Getting up off the floor requires assistance.

I guess it will not be over until "the fat lady sings", and she has seemed to have lost her voice. A few more things have occurred that are worth mentioning, and we are now within a week of a Presidential Election that might go down as one of the most contested in terms of money, (billions), dirty politics, and results. It is now late October of 2020 and I find myself on the homeowners "problem guy" list with two strikes against me. The first strike was the signs issue and the most recent involved placing an eighteen inch high screen under the length of our golf cart garage door to improve air circulation during the hot summer days in our poorly designed garage. Our across-the-street neighbor had designed and installed this device to correct the air flow problem and helped my next-door neighbor and I me to do likewise. The Homeowners Association claimed we had not sought out their approval and demanded its removal. My two neighbors complied, but I held out until the last day of the demand, and have since kept the garage door raised eighteen inches (it looks just like the screen) in protest.

Growing Old in America

A few weeks ago, Sandy decided to accompany me on a five mile walk and, upon returning to the house some ninety minutes later, walked into a house with partially flooded engineered hardwood floors. She had been washing something in the laundry room deep sink before we left and left the water running. The sink does not have an overflow drain and overflowed to partially flood the house. Since the flooring is not made any longer, it all has to be replaced. This would have been a monumental task as all the furniture would have to be packed and removed, the existing floor and baseboards removed from its glued-down application on the cement floor, the glue removed from the slab, and new flooring installed. We would to have moved out during the process and spend countless hours cleaning up the dust from the process. This would be the second time the hardwood floors would have to be replaced, with the first time due to the builder's problem. In researching new flooring, we found a vinyl simulated hardwood that was waterproof and could be overlaid onto the existing floor, thus eliminating tearing up the existing floor. It was also considerably less expensive than what the insurance paid us for the settlement. The installation is scheduled for the first week in November. The amazing thing is that five other neighbors within one hundred yards of us have had the same flooding experience with their laundry room sink.

Speaking of amazing. While playing golf with the Hackers recently, I played in a foursome that included someone I had not played with before, and in the course of introduction found out he was from my hometown of Hastings-on-Hudson and was ten years behind me graduation from my school. His family had also gravitated from Yonkers to Hastings and he was familiar with the Nepera Park neighborhood and our location next to School 22. Even more amazing was his family used to go to the tavern we lived next to in Hastings, Rushnaks and Zooks, for sandwiches, but I was long gone by then.

Megan and David have decided to come down to Canton for Thanksgiving and were originally going to fly. Megan called recently to say they had decided to drive down to limit their exposure to Covid and our subsequent exposure to them. The damn virus is on the increase again locally, nationally, and globally. She also announced that she had completed her first year anniversary at the National Institute of Health and had received a $20,000 pay increase, going from step 1 in her pay grade to step 10, the highest step, and pushed her up to $103,000. This is after the $3000 increase she received when Trump gave a pay increase to all Federal employees earlier in the year. Megan said she has never made so much money for doing so little work. Only in the Federal Government!

As I may have mentioned before, this epistle has turned into a diary of sorts with no apparent end in sight. Hopefully, there is more to come but that remains to be seen. On page one I compared my body to a machine and marveled that few machines lasted 65 years. As of the close of this book on December 15th, 2020, my bucket of bolts has lasted 81 years and 115 days.

Life goes on! Today is January first of 2021. Another year added to my resume. Trump has lost the election and never conceded, and the Republicans are in danger of losing the Senate from a run-off election next week for two Georgia Republican Senators. The country has been governed by partisan politics the past twenty years with no end in sight.

MicroSoft has crashed on my old computer and I almost lost this book. It must be a sign to end this thing. My golf/drinking/poker player neighbor Bob says I should do a fourth book and call it "Growing Older In America". Sorry Bob, but this is it.

EPILOGUE

Having become disenchanted with their careers in Health Care, the Filkowski husband and wife team decided to pursue their dream of owning and operating a Country Inn or Bed and Breakfast. They exhausted all possibilities of doing so in California and pursued opportunities back East with numerous site visits; finally finding an up and running operation that met their life-style criteria. It took eight years to renovate, reorganize, and recoup their investment before realizing that a seven day-twenty four hour existence was taking a toll on Walt's sixty-five year old body. Their exit strategy from Innkeeping centered on their kids and grandkids, with a final move to the Atlanta, Georgia, area winning out over a return to California. As they found out to be the case later, along with a majority of their senior age friends, following your kids/grandkids strategy has its shortcomings.

Their "final" move was to Big Canoe, a mountain community ninety minutes away from daughter Lauri and her family in Peachtree City; and daughter Megan, who was attending Emory University in Atlanta. During the next nine years in Big Canoe, younger wife Sandy returned to work, daughter Lauri and the two grandsons moved to Australia and then to California, daughter Megan moves first to Dartmouth College in New Hampshire, then back to Atlanta, then to Athens, Georgia, then to Houston. So much for following your kids!

The "final" move to Big Canoe proved to be not final and when wife Sandy decided to retire from her job after eight years, a decision was made to return to California and be close to Sandy's brother and the other two kids, Dana, and Scott, and the twin grandsons. A house was ordered built in a Del Webb community near Palm Springs and the Big Canoe house sold in a declining real estate market. This "final" move to California was cancelled, as it took place, by Walt having a heart "episode" during the move, with the result being a revised "final" move to an over 55 gated community in nearby Canton, Georgia.

This "final" move has lasted seven years with Walt at the age of 81 and Sandy at age 71. This has been where growing old has manifested itself in terms of deteriorating healthcare and experience being part of the "sandwich generation" , whereby you find yourself dealing with both your parents\older siblings problems and your own children's problems. Walt has outlived his three siblings now and his parents are long gone, but Sandy still has to deal with her schizophrenic younger brother and his two wayward daughters. Her parents are also deceased so that removes one half of the sandwich, and the combined family children and grandchildren seem to be doing o.k., with a few minor glitches.

"Growing Old" seems to have developed into waking up and going through the old person routine until bed time. Who knows how long his will go on, but it is no longer interesting enough to write about.

www.ingramcontent.com/pod-product-compliance
Lightning Source LLC
Chambersburg PA
CBHW060517100426
42743CB00009B/1348